Life After Easter

Easter is literally just behind us – so what comes next. As we wish to follow Jesus through ministry, betrayal, death and resurrection, we cannot expect to live in the same way as we did before.

Brian Radcliffe ends his studies in Mark's Gospel with a challenge: 'The next chapter belongs to us.' The ending of Mark is blunt and mysterious and does not give us the details we'd like about what Jesus' followers did next. The first disciples had to work it out – and so do we.

Thankfully, we have three things the early believers did not have in those first days after Easter. We have the gift of the Holy Spirit in our lives – the power of God to sustain us and enlighten us. We have brothers and sisters in our churches to support and encourage us. We have the written Word of God to guide us – not just the Old Testament but also the New: the powerful and life-changing reflections on the resurrection of Jesus that have been set down for us by other faithful followers as stories, letters and revelations.

I love the way our writers have opened up for us the life and light of God shining through these readings. 1 Chronicles is presented as sermons for life, not history; Deuteronomy as 'our Lord's favourite book', delighting in the Law; Acts as a journey of faithful witness; John as setting out the choice of life or death that we make when we respond to Christ; and Galatians as setting the bar high for our life together.

We also start our new series, *Light for My Path*, in this issue. We concluded the basic Bible-reading series, *Bible Unpacked*, in the last quarter, and this next series will introduce us to the way in which the Bible has impacted the lives of some of our note writers and SU staff. It is a privilege to listen in on how God has used his Word in their lives, and we are grateful for their willingness to share with us.

Sally Nelson
Editor

Isaac O'Brien
Content Assistant

ON THE COVER: '… the Lord … took me out of the bog I was in and set my feet on a rock, putting a new song in my mouth.' (pages 66 to 69; cf Ps 40:1–3)

Image credit: Shutterstock / sharptoyou

The Writers

BRIAN RADCLIFFE is a retired English and Drama teacher, and formerly a minister of a Baptist church in the north of England. He also enjoys a parallel career as a freelance writer (writing secondary assembly scripts/drama skills as cross-curricular teaching tools).

HOWARD PESKETT was Vice Principal at Trinity College, Bristol, UK, where he taught mission and religion. He served with Overseas Missionary Fellowship in Singapore for 20 years until he retired in 2006.

JONNY LIBBY is the Lay Pastor at Plymouth Methodist Central Hall. This role includes being the Methodist Chaplain at the University of Plymouth.

VIVIEN WHITFIELD is retired, but is still serving as a minister in her local church. Her past includes mission service in Peru with Latin Link, Deaf ministry, and tutoring Extension Studies theological students with St Johns College, Nottingham, UK.

TANYA FERDINANDUSZ is both a freelance writer and freelance editor, and has been writing Bible reading notes, articles and devotionals for over 25 years. She is a Bible Study leader and the author of *Marriage Matters*, a book for Christian couples.

PETER S C POTHAN is a Bible teacher and theologian who was called by God to teach for over 50 years in India and abroad. He has written 51 self-study theological courses plus some booklets and magazine articles. Now retired, Peter still teaches Distance Learning students.

SALLY NELSON is the Dean of Baptist Formation at St Hild College, Yorkshire, UK, where she also teaches Christian doctrine and pastoral care. She is a Baptist minister and has been the commissioning editor for *Encounter with God* since 2015.

ISAAC O'BRIEN is a Content Assistant at Scripture Union and the content manager of *Encounter with God*. He is passionate about the Bible, theology and Jesus, and loves leading worship in church.

Contents

Scripture Union is a member of the worldwide Scripture Union international community.
Website: https://scriptureunion.global

PATIENCE PAYS OFF

Despite serious health issues in his retirement years, Roger Purdom has become a Faith Guide and continues to introduce young people to Jesus. He shares some of his story, and talks about the importance of building relationships and why we all have a vital role to play in building the church of today and tomorrow.

Roger has had a long association with Scripture Union; he went on his first SU camp in Arthog near Barmouth in 1964. Later he became an SU team leader, helping on different holidays until 1981.

For many years, he was a teacher at a school in Croydon, and ran SU holiday clubs at the church where he was an elder.

Then he moved to East Sussex to take up the headship of a Christian boarding school. He began his final job in 1995 as pastor of an independent church in Littlehampton. Roger recalls, 'We launched summer holiday clubs at church, using SU resources, and I did those until I

retired. Each year we had sixty to seventy children attending.'

The break that got Roger into schools
When Roger first moved to Littlehampton, he wanted to do Christian assemblies in schools, but initially there was quite a bit of resistance. The break came when one school heard that he was trained as an OFSTED inspector. 'In those days, spirituality was one of the aspects that OFSTED inspected. The school asked if I'd come and do Christian assemblies to help them pass their forthcoming inspection.

'Word got around; soon I was going into ten primary schools. Those doors have never closed, not even during COVID! Instead they asked me to do assemblies on Zoom. That suited me too because by then I'd developed some quite serious health issues.' Even so, Roger has managed to do over one hundred assemblies in the past two years.

'The kids know I'm going to tell them a Bible story and pray, but I usually get a positive reaction and a listening ear from them.

'I hope to get back into schools eventually, but for now the doors are still open and I'm still doing Zoom.'

Sharing his testimony

'One head at a C of E school asked if I could do some sessions on the Trinity and prayer. Afterwards, he said, "The kids loved it, so now can you do some sessions on characters in the Bible whose faith was tested but God brought them through?" So I did Ruth, Esther, Mary, Peter and others.

'Then he asked, "Can you talk about how your faith has been tested and how God has brought you through?" I did three sessions: one on when I was a teenager and first came to faith, one on my teaching years and one on my church pastor years.

'These talks were also publicised in emails to parents, and when my wife went into a local shop an assistant said, "Oh, the kids love Roger and his assemblies!"'

Camp always oversubscribed!

In 2003, Roger started a summer camp for local children. 'We took them to the beach – it was a first for many of them, even though they lived so close by,' Roger recalls. 'We played games; they got

soaking wet and filthy dirty and had an incredible time!

'Eventually we had to move. We relocated about ten miles inland to Lodge Hill, an activity centre. During the day, the kids would do all sorts of adventurous stuff which they loved – abseiling, mountain biking, climbing. In the morning and evening we'd have Bible stories, worship and a talk.

'Out of the 60 children already booked on to this year's camp, about 90 per cent won't have heard a Bible story other than ones we might have shared at an assembly. Parents know it's Christian, but every year we are oversubscribed.'

The domino effect

Roger recognises the enormous value of building relationships. 'If you want to draw children into a relationship with God, you have to first build a relationship with them. And by connecting with them in different situations – school, camp, church – you get to know not just the kids but the parents and teachers too.

'It's vital to build genuine friendships across the community, seeking to serve that community. It's not just about what *you* want – what will *they* value? One time the churches in Littlehampton did a meal for head teachers at the end of each academic year to thank them for what they do with the children and young people in our area, and for allowing us to partner them on that journey.

'While we serve, we are so often blessed. One church in our Littlehampton group was in a little village called Lyminster. When its new curate started a family service, it had a great response and attracted families from much further afield because they knew us from camps and assemblies.

'It's like a domino effect: all those different contact points are interlinked.'

The value of church volunteers

It takes time and patience to build those genuine community-wide relationships. 'That's why I feel ordinary church members of all ages have a vital part to play,' Roger says. 'If the relationship only resides with the church leader or youth

frightening. And the world is changing so fast that we can't keep up with the trends.

'More than ever, young people need to hear that God is there for them, that he loves them and that he will never, ever change – he's the same today and for ever.'

Please pray for Roger and all Faith Guides as they commit their time and skills to helping children and young people to learn more about God. If you would like to know more about becoming a Faith Guide, visit su.org.uk/faithguides.

worker, it can falter if those people move on, which they often do. Not all church leaders have the skills or experience to work with young people either.'

Becoming a Faith Guide through SU really helps those church volunteers who are taking that role, as Roger has found. 'It recognises that this is a long-term process, and provides training, encouragement and access to resources.' There is also the opportunity to network with and learn from other Faith Guides.

Roger plans to keep sharing the good news of Jesus with children and young people for as long as God enables him to do so. 'We mustn't give up on the next generation. What kids are being exposed to via their phones, computers and TV is

A shorter version of this story first appeared in *Connecting You*, SU's free quarterly supporter magazine. If you'd like to receive copies of *Connecting You* and learn more of how God is moving in the hearts and lives of children and young people today, you can sign up online at su.org.uk/connectingyou.

Using this Guide

Encounter with God is designed for thinking Christians who want to interpret and apply the Bible in a way that is relevant to the problems and issues of today's world. It is based on the NIV translation of the Bible, but can easily be used with any other version.

Each set of readings begins with an *Introduction* to the section you are about to study. The *Call to Worship* section at the start of each note should help you consciously to come into God's presence before you read the passage. The main *Explore* section aims to bring out the riches hidden in the text. The *Growing in Faith* section at the end suggests ways of applying the message to daily living.

The *Bible in a Year* readings at the foot of the page are for those who want this additional option.

THE WEEK THAT CHANGED THE WORLD

The first readers of (or listeners to) Mark's Gospel didn't have the luxury of four Gospels to compare with each other. For the largely Gentile audience, probably living in Rome, this was the first organised account of the life, death and resurrection of Jesus. It reads like a series of video shorts, actions taking priority over words, deeds over teaching. Based on the experience of Peter, there's a first-hand vividness to the Gospel. It's frank and honest, particularly in relation to the highs and lows of Peter's role, but with Jesus central to every episode.

Chapters 11 to 16 of Mark encompass the final phase of the account. In the earlier chapters we have seen Jesus' early Galilean ministry and the enigmatic excursions into northern Palestine. The disciples have been called and trained. Everything then hinges on Peter's confession in chapter 8, the recognition that Jesus is the promised Messiah. From this point on, the direction of the action turns south towards Jerusalem, with the departure from Galilee. The men and women from the north approach the capital.

Chapters 1 to 10 of the Gospel have been selective, covering three years of Jesus' ministry. They read like the edited highlights of an eventful time. By contrast, chapters 11 to 16 give a day by day, often hour by hour, account of a single week. Miracles are few. Instead, it's a time of controversies, some initiated by Jesus, others the work of the religious and legal authorities, threatened by the powerful presence of Jesus in a city already overcrowded by the influx of pilgrims for the Passover festival. The climax is devastating, an abyss of injustice, torture and death quietly transformed in a garden early one morning. Just as Jesus said it would be.

Brian Radcliffe

Mark 16:9–20

Seeing is Believing

Lord, Easter is amazing. How do you follow that? Draw me into your mission, please.

Yesterday's reading felt somehow unfinished, lacking a denouement to the Jesus story. Three frightened women fled – but who knows where? Mark's early audiences knew that it didn't end like that. Today's passage is missing from some manuscripts, but it is important as a transition to the era that includes us. If it reads like a brief summary of Luke/Acts, then that's because it unifies the experience of the early church.

Mary Magdalene is the one who eventually takes the surprising news to Jesus' followers. Do they greet it with overwhelming joy? Not a chance (see v 11): 'Please, Mary, we know you mean well but...'. A report by two disciples of an encounter on a country road fares no better (v 13). It takes a manifestation to the whole inner group, accompanied by a rebuke from Jesus, to convince the remaining eleven (v 14). Turning the situation round, Jesus then commissions them to take this same gloriously unlikely message to the whole world of cynical and doubting humanity. Now, however, signs and wonders will accompany the gospel that they, and we, are to take (vs 17,18). If people then don't believe, be it on their own heads (v 16).

Is this the end (v 19)? Well, not exactly, for the story never ends. We've read the next events in Acts and followed the legends of the saints down through the centuries. Now, in 2024, this is our truth: Jesus, who was raised to life and ascended into heaven, is still seated at the right hand of God. His story of salvation is the same. His Spirit inspires us and our audiences with words, healings and wonders. The next chapter belongs to us.

How does your next chapter begin? Read again Jesus' commission (vs 15–18) as if addressed to you (as it actually is!) and look forward to the day ahead.

BIBLE IN A YEAR: **Joshua 1–3; Psalm 37**

Deuteronomy 1:1 – 16:17

MOSES' CALL TO LOVE THE LORD ALONE

We begin our post-Easter journey with one of our Lord's favourite books – Deuteronomy. If I have one hour, I read chapters 1–11 out loud (or listen to David Suchet, for example, reading them in the NIVUK audio version). If time is lacking, I begin by reading Psalm 19:7–11 and Matthew 5:17–20, which remind me of Jewish delight in the Law – its piercing quality like the Middle Eastern sun. This is why there is a mezuzah on the doorpost of every pious Jewish home, which residents brush with their fingers every time they leave and enter.

I imagine myself gathered with ancient listeners and many modern readers to hear Moses' last will and testament, as a description of my inheritance; everything our beloved leader wants us to remember, cherish and embody. Chapters 1–4 set the scene, with many reminders from the Torah's earlier books; chapters 5–11 set out the basic framework of the covenant, including the first passage which every Jewish child learns. Then we plunge into the first part of the detailed legislation which will govern the shape, texture and ethos of Jewish community life – because a *nation* is in the process of formation; history is being made.

I prepare for a turbulent ride these three weeks. The book has a sermonic quality and all the biggest words in the Old Testament are here – the LORD, awesome in love, majesty, judgement, fire, anger and mercy. The people of God, corrupt, stiff-necked, grumbling, listening, promising, forgetting, obeying, hoping, fearing. Moses the prophet, teacher, intercessor, mediator, man of sorrows. And chilling words – destroy, wipe out, no pity, conquer. I implore the help of the Holy Spirit as I read, eager to make my way to 'a land flowing with milk and honey'.[1]

Howard Peskett

FOR FURTHER READING

C Wright, *Deuteronomy*, Hendrickson, 1996
J Sacks, *Covenant and Conversation*, Maggid Books, 2017
H Painter, *God of Violence Yesterday, God of Love Today?*, BRF, 2019
https://bibleproject.com/explore/video/deuteronomy/

[1] Eg Exod 3:8; Deut 27:3

A Liminal Place

I sit quietly and breathe deeply for a few moments. Am I a grateful person? Am I quick to judge or to complain? Am I passionate about justice?

For Jewish people, Moses is, above all, *Moshe Rabbeinu*, Moses our Teacher. Deuteronomy contains his last words (the book ends with the account of his death). We would certainly pay special attention to a loved person's words if we knew that they would be their last. Am I myself in a liminal place too? 'Liminal' means on the boundary; on a threshold; in a transitional state between X and Y. Am I facing a change, a future with many unknowns, the dissolution of old certainties? I will make my pilgrimage through this book into a review-and-revision session.

To know which way to go, I need to know where I am starting. Place names (v 1), chronological data and a description of 'the land' (vs 7,8) feature in today's reading; together with a tantalising reminder that an eleven days' journey has somehow taken forty years (vs 2,3). These are fascinating details for another sort of study.

Today's reading focuses on legacy, on delegation of leadership. What picture of Moses' community do I glimpse behind his brief description in verse 12? What are the particular qualities that Moses looks for in his 'judges' or 'leaders' (vs 15–18)? I think with special care about what lies behind the words 'judge righteously' (v 16, ASV): 'Do not show partiality … Do not be afraid of anyone … Bring me any case too hard for you' (v 17, NIV). I notice, too, that small and great, brother and alien are to be treated fairly. I think about my own society, the judgers and the judged. We cannot have a decent society without justice; but the justice must also be 'righteous' – this word is prominent in Genesis and in Deuteronomy, the bookends of the Torah.

How can I make things more just for everybody, where I live or work? Do I speak up when things are not done properly? I pray for courage, for wisdom.

BIBLE IN A YEAR: Joshua 4,5; Romans 10

Dithering

Am I a decisive person or do I dither, vacillate, procrastinate? Does this question itself make me dither? What would my most faithful friend say? What might God say?

Moses reflects on events set out more fully in Numbers 13 and 14. I do not go to that passage unless I have to. Instead, I focus on the verbs (the action words) through which this section unfolds. Phase 1: 'Go up' (v 21) – What incentives are given? Phase 2: '[We are] unwilling to go up' (v 26); how outrageous is the Israelites' grumbling here? Phase 3: Who feels the force of God's anger (v 37)? Phase 4: 'We will go up' (v 41); I note the word 'arrogance' (v 43). Phase 5: What happens to the Israelites? And how does God respond? What vivid language in this passage makes me catch my breath? God as a warrior? As a father carrying his child? '... the LORD ... solemnly swore' (v 34). '... the LORD ... paid no attention' (v 45).

The Old Testament speaks vigorously of God's form (eyes, mouth, face, arms, hands), God's feelings (loves, laughs, repents, is angry, glad) and God's actions (sees, hears, speaks, rests, smells, swears) in language that is almost embarrassingly direct at times. This so-called anthropomorphic language is used so that we might understand that God is the *personal living God*. He is not just a vast pile of abstractions or concepts, protected by limitless definitions. He is contrasted with idols who hear nothing, see nothing, do nothing, *are* nothing.

I conclude my meditation on this passage by returning to verse 31. If I have a cross-referencing Bible it may direct me to Exodus 19:4, Isaiah 46:3 and Hosea 11:3. I steady my wobbling, juddering self with renewed joy in God's steadfast, carrying love.

Some people are steady in their discipleship; others are mercurial. Which are more prone to dithering? Where am I among these people? I pray for stability, for steadiness.

Momentous Decisions

Sensitise my heart, Lord, that I may know when critical moments come and that I may be ready to follow your directions precisely and fully.

The Israelites have been wandering in the wilderness 'long enough' (v 3). Now it is time to turn north. I note the words, 'Do *not*' and 'Do *not* harass' (see vs 9,19) – and, later, the Israelites *are* to contend with Sihon king of Heshbon (v 24). There are more details about these events in Numbers 20 and 21; a map may help with place names, not all of which are certain.

An underlying theme of these encounters with Edom, Moab, Ammon, Sihon and Og, not particularly emphasised but important for the missionary relevance of Deuteronomy, is the sovereignty of God over all these nations. Even in the passages which the publishers have put in brackets, such as the settlement of Caphtorites (from Crete?) in the region of Gaza (v 23), God is somehow at work. I refresh my heart with this assurance in the midst of the turbulence of my own world.

The battle with Sihon is a turning point (v 25). There are echoes of the Pharaoh story (v 30): the Lord had turned his eliminating hand against his own disobedient people in the wilderness (vs 14,15); and now Sihon's people, despite their cities' high walls (v 36, NRSV) were also going to experience the Lord's judgement. The language of verse 34 is the language of a war report: it uses total-kill hyperbole and simplification. The Israelites have already been told that the land they are to possess is ready to vomit the Canaanites out;[1] and they are repeatedly reminded that it is Canaanite wickedness not Israelite righteousness which has led to the dispossession.[2]

I pray for those who suffer from evil deeds and for those who seek to bring these evils to an end. I pray that God may sharpen my own conscience.

[1] Lev 18:24–30 [2] Deut 9:5

BIBLE IN A YEAR: **Joshua 8,9; Romans 12**

Disappointments

I reflect on how I handle disappointments in my life and ask for more grace and steadiness.

Today's passage falls into three sections. In the first (vs 1–11), King Og of Bashan experiences the same treatment as Sihon king of Heshbon. Thus the 'two kings of the Amorites' (v 8) were despatched. I take note of at least seven hyperbolic expressions in verses 3–7, the stereotyped language of a war report, as yesterday. The editor adds some details of geography and nomenclature and a note about king Og's giant bed in vs 9–11.

Verses 12–22 then summarise a somewhat heated discussion in Numbers 32 about the inheritances of Reuben, Gad and Manasseh, east of the Jordan. If my Bible has a map, I will be able to get a general impression of these territories, without certainty about all the places. The division between the tribes east and west of the Jordan was to cause some trouble later. Deborah's song criticised those who would not help her in her battles, including some east Jordanian tribes.[1] God, however, will continue to lead through Joshua, who is given a renewed promise in verse 22.[2]

Finally, Moses makes the Lord impatient (v 26) by asking again if he may be permitted to enter the 'good land' (vs 23–27). Here and elsewhere,[3] it seems as if the people are to blame for his exclusion, but other texts suggest it was something in Moses' own provocative behaviour that led to this disappointment.[4] God's refusal – 'you are not going to cross this Jordan' (v 27) – is, however, moderated by an instruction – 'Look at the land with your own eyes' – which strikingly echoes his promise to Abraham![5] Readers of the Bible's big story will recall that, much later, Moses *did* appear on a mountain top inside the good land, discussing with the Lord Jesus the biggest exodus of all.[6]

How can I assess Moses' disappointments, or my own? I resolve to keep running my race with eyes fixed on Jesus, my Forerunner.

[1] Judg 5:15-17 [2] See Exod 14:14 [3] Deut 1:37; 4:21; Ps 106:32,33 [4] Num 20; Deut 32:45-52 [5] Gen 13:14 [6] Luke 9:30,31

BIBLE IN A YEAR: **Joshua 10,11; Psalm 38**

A Jealous, Zealous God

Our Lord resisted Satan's temptations with three quotes from Deuteronomy.[1] What words am I going to store in my heart for harder times?

First, I reflect on the Voice (v 12): 'The word which I command you' (v 2, literally); and 'The Ten Words' (v 13, literally). What is the difference between a religion of the eye and one of the ear? Why does Moses emphasise that there was no visible form (v 12) at Mount Horeb? Why is idolatry so firmly forbidden?

Second, I observe the seven mentions of fire in this chapter. Verse 24, 'God is a consuming fire', is quoted in Hebrews.[2] See also, 'I am very jealous for Zion; I am burning with jealousy for her'.[3] At Christmas time a common reading from Isaiah speaks of the Messiah's coming kingdom and finishes with 'The zeal of the LORD Almighty will accomplish this'.[4] The Lord is passionate about the fidelity of Israel, his covenanted spouse. What am I jealous about? Zealous about? What matters most to me in matters of faith and loyalty? How do I distinguish a proper zeal from personal anger?

Third, this chapter reminds me that the Lord is a merciful God (v 31). It is in the nature of fire to warm as well as to burn. The Israelites have the capacity to turn at any moment off the track of covenantal obedience. The mercy and forgiveness of God are therefore always, repeatedly a wonder, a surprise, a benediction! This chapter several times mentions children and grandchildren. It is in Deuteronomy that the word 'lamad', to teach or to learn, appears for the first time (v 1).[5] Long before there were formal schools of any sort, the Jewish family was itself a school where children learned faith, worship and obedience. It is said today that by the age of seven many children have already decided whether or not they will follow the faith they have been taught.

I pray for children and grandchildren, my own if I have any, and other youngsters and young people.

---

[1] Luke 4:4,8,12; Deut 8:3; 6:13,16 [2] Heb 12:29 [3] Zech 8:2 [4] Isa 9:7 [5] See also Deut 6:7,20–25; 11:19; the word is not used in Genesis, Exodus, Leviticus or Numbers

BIBLE IN A YEAR: **Joshua 12–15; Romans 13**

Psalm 131

Stilled and Quieted

Heart, eyes, soul – I bring them all to quietness before the Lord.

CH Spurgeon wrote that this psalm was one of the shortest to read and one of the longest to learn. Breastfeeding is a most precious gift that a mother gives to her child, who knows only the law of demand and supply – and that law's instrument, which is crying. There comes a time, however, when the child must be weaned; it cannot remain for ever at the breast. David pictures his headstrong self, sitting contentedly, like child and mother side by side. There are some ironies in the psalm, when I remember the actual course of David's middle and later life. Am I in charge of my heart, my eyes, my soul? Can I bring them to quietness? Fear of missing out and incessant distraction dog my life. If I am getting older, it may feel like a diminishment, but for a child the denial and loss of the breast is the gateway to a *fuller* life. I sit quietly this very minute.

Verse 1 deals with unruly ambition. Verse 2 deals with children's dependence. David does not have too low an opinion of others. He does not have too high an opinion of himself. His life is in full flow – in Psalm 130 he is watching and waiting for mercy; Psalm 132 pictures a major task of finding a suitable place for the ark of God. In between and throughout these tasks, there is a need for David and for Israel to put their hope and trust in the Lord. The Lord is the first word of Psalm 131 and its final resting-place. Whatever tasks, long-term or short-term, are facing me, I take today, this sabbath, this day of rest, to quieten my soul and receive strength for these tasks.

Is there something that I must learn to do without? I renew my contentment and hope that God is working all things together for my good.

BIBLE IN A YEAR: **Joshua 16–19; Romans 14**

Deuteronomy 5:1–21

Ten Great Freedoms

Culture rests on cult; values presuppose beliefs. I pray for myself and for my society for a clearer understanding of how beliefs and behaviour interact.

I reflect quietly on the Ten Commandments. Do I know them by heart? From childhood? Philip Rieff, an American writer on philosophy and social ethics, wrote that 'a culture is known by the behaviour it forbids'. Do I agree with this assertion? Why should it be so? Deuteronomy 1–4 set out the context for this final great Mosaic statement. Chapters 5–11 set out the heart of the covenant, before chapters 12–26 lay out detailed legislation. I take note of the initial words, 'Hear … Learn … follow'. A generation had passed away since God's original covenant had been made with the Israelites at Mount Horeb, but Moses insists that the covenant is with us – us who are here alive today (v 3). Moses also highlights his own mediatorial role (v 5). I thank God if I had someone who mediated to me the knowledge of God while I was still young.

Many people who have a superficial knowledge of the Bible summarise the Old Testament as 'law' and the New Testament as 'grace' – but the Ten Words *begin with redemption* in verse 6. The commandments that follow and which are to shape Israel's life include a focus on the rescue from slavery in Egypt by God's mighty hand and outstretched arm (v 15). I repeat the Ten Words to myself slowly, pausing on each one. I remember how the Lord Jesus did not abolish these laws but instead intensified them. The rules of a game give freedom to the game and pleasure to the spectators; if you buy an expensive piece of electronic equipment it will come with the manufacturer's instructions – it is in the keeping of these instructions that you will enjoy your purchase fully. A famous prayer includes the words 'whose service is perfect freedom'.[1]

Penitently, I pray for God's forgiveness for when I have broken his commandments. Boldly, I pray that I and my society may (re)discover the freedom which these laws bring.

---

[1] Collect for Peace, Morning Prayer, *The Book of Common Prayer*

BIBLE IN A YEAR: **Joshua 20–22; Psalm 39**

Deuteronomy 5:22-33

We Will Hear and Do It

I give thanks for men and women everywhere who hear the Word of God and *do* it – putting into practice what they hear, sometimes with very slender resources.

My imagination awakes as I picture the scene when the Law was given by God – the fire, the cloud, the thick darkness, the earthquake, the loud voice and the writing. Many Israelites thought, in those days, that to see God was to die.[1] The assembly begs Moses to mediate for them (I note the word 'all' in verse 27) and they vow that they will hear the word of the Lord and do it. Do I have a comparable sense of wonder and joy that, through the Bible and the Holy Spirit, I have a *revelation* from God? Psalm 119 spends 176 verses extolling the wonders of the laws, the statutes, the ordinances. David in Psalm 19 writes of the heavens declaring the glory of God and compares the 'law of the LORD' to the sun, which warms all the earth. Once a year the Jews celebrate the giving of the Law on the day called '*Simchat Torah*'. The sacred scrolls are taken out of their ark and the people dance with joy, often for several hours. It is a joy, a wonder that there is a living God and he has spoken to us.

The Lord is pleased with the Israelites' response (vs 28,29), but he has a realistic understanding of the people's frailties. I trace, one by one, the verbs used in verses 29–33 which, then and now, expand and deepen our understanding of what walking in the ways of the Lord really means.

I conclude my meditation by focusing on the words 'be careful to do' (v 32), a phrase that recurs throughout the book of Deuteronomy. Here I am reading the Bible today; perhaps I do this every day; I may even be quite knowledgeable about what the Bible says. However...

What steps am I taking today and every day to 'be careful to do' everything that I hear from and know about God and his will and ways?

---

[1] Judg 13:22; Isa 6:5

BIBLE IN A YEAR: **Joshua 23,24; Romans 15**

Deuteronomy 6

Love the Lord your God

I search my heart to see if verse 5 is true for me. If the fire has dimmed, how may it be rekindled?

Like an intricate fugue, three themes interweave in this chapter: (1) God's commandments, laws, decrees, stipulations; (2) what the Lord has done and will do for and to his people; and (3) lots of verbs describing how the people are to respond to God. I trace these themes, perhaps with a coloured pen. I remember that Jesus battled Satan with two verses from this chapter (vs 13,16)[1] and that here he found also the greatest commandment (v 5).[2]

Verses 4 and 5 are the first words of the Torah which a Jewish child learns. Listen! God is the Lord. He is the only God. We are to love him totally, with all our heart and soul and 'muchness' (literally). This is the plumb line running through Jewish life. Love is commanded – so it is not just a feeling which may come or go. It denotes obedience, loyalty, reverence – and it is linked with fearing God too (v 24),

with which it is completely compatible. It is assumed (v 7) that this is a family matter which is talked about at home with children and grandchildren; many Jews still have a mezuzah on their door frame; not so many have a phylactery on their foreheads. It is more important, though, to have these words bound on my heart[3] than on my arm or neck or head. What is my faith-gift to my children and grandchildren, if I have any, or to any youngsters who are near to me?

I conclude by echoing the thanks of this chapter for all the wonderful gifts that God has given to me, especially those Christians who have helped me on my own pilgrimage.

Pray for wisdom about how we read verses 10–12 in the light of the current difficult situation in the Holy Land.

---

[1] Luke 4:8,12 [2] Matt 22:37 [3] Prov 6:20-22

BIBLE IN A YEAR: **Judges 1,2; Romans 16**

Destruction – and Love

Lord, where my understanding lacks, teach me by your Holy Spirit, that I might gain new understanding.

This chapter talks of total destruction (eg v 2) and God's electing love. The extermination language cannot be taken too literally, as is demonstrated by the forbidding of intermarriage, the curious language about 'the hornet' (v 20) and the slow conquest, the seven nations and the book of Joshua. The major concern of the chapter is the temptation to worship false gods. Detailed instructions are given about how to prevent this. The whole Old Testament story shows how this was a constant danger.

In the middle of this violent and frightening language are the most wonderful explanations of how 'God loves you because he loves you', how he is a covenant-keeping God and how the Israelites will be the most blessed of all peoples. I trace the details – carefully.

Three early acts of judgement by God in the Pentateuch are made without human agency: the flood; the destruction of Sodom; and the plagues of Egypt. It appears that there are times when God says, 'Enough! That's it!' and judgement falls. Jesus spoke of this[1] and Revelation is full of songs and sorrows and judgements. Reading the bigger story confirms to us that this chapter is not about xenophobia or genocide: Rahab the Canaanite was saved; Achan the Israelite and his family were destroyed. The chapter places before me the absolute priority of faithfulness to the God who has chosen me and his abhorrence of anything that will shift me from my allegiance to him. The choosing of Abraham and his descendants was not an act of favouritism but a stage in the intention of God to bless all nations.[2] Before we entertain any jealous thoughts about God's choice of the Jews, we need to remember how much they have suffered.

Lord, may I be faithful to your fervent love for me, without pride but with deep humility and gratitude; committing myself to serve others for your sake.

[1] Eg Matt 7:23; 25:46 [2] Gen 12

BIBLE IN A YEAR: **Judges 3,4; Proverbs 1,2**

Deuteronomy 8

Look Back – and Forward

I let the words 'you will lack nothing' (v 9) reverberate in my heart.

I review the various verbs used in this chapter to describe what the Lord has done to Israel in the past: led, humble, test, causing you to hunger, feeding you, disciplines. What are the most important lessons God wanted Israel to learn in that 'vast and dreadful wilderness' (v 15)? How does this explain Jesus' use of verse 3 in his conflict in the desert with Satan?[1] I turn to reflect on my own life. Have I experienced hard times, 'that thirsty and waterless land, with its venomous snakes and scorpions' (v 15)? With hindsight, how do I sum up the contribution of those hard times to my discipleship? Have I also experienced the provision of clothes that did not wear out and unswollen feet (v 4)?

I observe the verbs describing the Israelites' future: be careful to follow, remember, observe, walking in obedience, praise the LORD your God, do not forget. The description of 'the good land' (vs 7,10) the Israelites are going to possess is rapturous, climaxing with 'you will lack nothing' (v 9). What dangers does the Lord foresee flowing from these times of plenty? The chapter ends by returning to the danger of idolatry – three times the bell tolls with the word 'destroyed' (vs 19,20). I turn to reflect on my own life. What particular threats have success and prosperity brought to my discipleship? Have pride and self-satisfaction drowned my zeal and extinguished my desire to pray?

I think about 'remembering'[2] and 'forgetting', words that occur like a refrain in Deuteronomy (and also in Psalms and Jeremiah). These are not just intellectual concepts in Deuteronomy. Remembering is to follow, to do, to obey; forgetting is to ignore or repudiate. Memory is the guardian of our consciences; and also the basis of our civilisations.

I pray for myself and my society; with gratitude for the 'good land' that God has given us; with penitence for pride, self-satisfaction and hardness of heart.

---

[1] Matt 4:4 [2] Eg Deut 5:15; 8:2; 9:7; 24:9; 25:17; 32:7

BIBLE IN A YEAR: **Judges 5,6; Psalms 40,41**

The Cost of Intercession

How serious am I in my intercessory praying? I pray for greater depth and greater sustainability.

Exodus 32–34 tells the original story on which this chapter reflects with selective detail. Three times the Lord warns Israel that their victory over the Anakites was not because of Israel's righteousness. I review the actual terms used of Israel in this story: stiff-necked, rebellious, corrupt, turned aside. Verses 22 and 23 throw in four other examples to add to the appalling story of what was going on at the bottom of Mount Horeb while Moses was at the top receiving the rules of the covenant which were to guide Israel. These emphases on the wickedness of the Anakites *and* the provocative idolatry of Israel are the spectacles through which we should view the conquest narrative. Does this story guide me in any confrontation with 'Anakites' in my own discipleship?

I use my remaining time to reflect on the picture given me in this chapter about Moses the intercessor. If I have a computer available I search for 'Michelangelo Moses' and look at the statue of Moses at San Pietro in Vincoli in Rome. What look like horns are probably the sculptor's attempt at rays of brightness. Moses was a *huge* figure as this chapter shows. In verse 14 the Lord says, 'Let me alone,' but Moses refuses to leave the Lord alone. He ignores the Lord's offer to make him a replacement for Abraham and funnel his promises in future through him, Moses. He argues with the Lord and finishes with a ninefold reminder in verses 26–29 that Israel is *his* people. Moses was a teacher;[1] he is called a prophet;[2] but here he is a suffering servant, flat on his face for days and nights at a time before the Lord, arguing, pleading, remonstrating, repudiating God's repudiation of his people. He prays for Aaron too, who cuts such a pathetic, cowardly figure in the story of the golden calf.[3]

Lord, help me to pray. Help me to begin to begin. Give me some daring in my prayers.

---

[1] Deut 5,6 [2] Deut 18:18 [3] Exod 32:24

BIBLE IN A YEAR: **Judges 7,8; Proverbs 3,4**

The Radiant Son of David

For what promises of the Lord am I still awaiting fulfilment?

This psalm is a meditation on 2 Samuel 6 and 7; if I have time I read Psalms 24 and 68 as well. I read this psalm carefully, noticing how the quotation marks focus on who is speaking. The same Hebrew phrase 'to/for David' in verses 1 and 17 brackets the psalm. Verses 2–9 record David's oath to the Lord and what happened next; verses 10–16 record the Lord's irrevocable oath to David and what that would involve. Finally, the pledge of verses 17 and 18 abundantly fulfils the plea of verse 1. I pause to renew my trust and hope that God will fulfil his promises to me beyond my expectations and even my imaginings.

The ark of God, symbol of his might and resting-place, had been neglected and almost lost in the fields of Jaar (v 6),[1] but David's plan, persisted in through disappointments and delays, was to find it a worthy home and worthy worshippers. Verse 10 suggests that David's successor, Solomon perhaps, was leading the joyful procession to Zion.

God's promise outstrips David's dedication. I count up to ten things that the Lord says he will do to/for David. King, princes, priests, poor and saints are all blessed. How wonderful that God's worshippers are what he desires. There is a 'horn' (v 17; symbolising a strong one, a king) and a lamp and a splendid crown – bringing to an end David's 'self-denial' (v 1) for ever. The next two psalms, Psalms 133 (the glorious unity of the saints) and 134 (their constant worship) bring this mini-collection of pilgrimage psalms, the 'Songs of Ascent', to a sumptuous close – but there are greater glories to follow for Christian worshippers as they hail 'great David's greater Son'.[2]

'... your kingdom come ... for yours is the kingdom and the power and the glory'.[3] I rejoice that there is a King and one day his majesty will be unveiled.

---

[1] See also 1 Chr 13:3 [2] James Montgomery, 1771–1854, 'Hail to the Lord's Anointed' [3] Matt 6:10,13

BIBLE IN A YEAR: **Judges 9,10; Proverbs 5,6**

He is Your Praise

I praise God from my heart, knowing, as I do, that I am only reaching the outskirts of his wonderful reality.

Moses is reaching the end of his long introduction (chs 5–11) to Deuteronomy. We are reminded that he received a new version of the Ten Commandments; there is a small digression on the death of Aaron (a sadder end than that of Moses); and a short excursion on the place of Levites in Israelite society.

Then Moses says, 'And now ...' (v 12, emphasis added) words commonly used in the Old Testament to introduce a summary. I read verses 12–22, slowly, several times, allowing them to reverberate in my memory since I have met so many of these words, especially the verbs, in previous chapters. I notice the words 'for your own good' in verse 13. A magazine article on the Ten Commandments was entitled 'Ten Great Freedoms'. These Ten Great Words do not slam us into a prison; they open us out into a garden. Moses insists that circumcision of the body is not enough – the badge of the covenant is not an external badge: it is a matter of the heart as Jeremiah and Paul later taught.[1]

Finally, I ponder verses 17 and 18. Rabbi Yohanan in the third century wrote a short homily on these verses which has passed into the Jewish liturgy for the end of *Shabbat*: even though God is so high and awe-inspiring he cares for the orphan, the widow, the stranger. This is found in the Prophets [2] and in the Psalms[3] as well. It is also, of course, a theme in the New Testament.[4] Is my behaviour God-like in this respect? Do I notice the low, the lost, the lonely?

Is there someone I should visit or call or write to? Not for my reputation, but because in order to worship God we must grow to be like him.

[1] Jer 4:4; Rom 2:28,29 [2] Eg Isa 57:15 [3] Eg Ps 68:5,6 [4] Eg Matt 5:3-12

BIBLE IN A YEAR: **Judges 11,12; Psalms 42,43**

A Land of Milk and Honey

Lord, I thank you for everything you have in store for me – beyond my deserving and often my desiring. Help me not to miss the way to these wonders.

At the centre of this chapter is another mouth-watering description of the Promised Land; there may even be a touch of humour in the description of it being watered directly from heaven, unlike the elaborate, man-made kitchen garden of Egypt. In the days before modern irrigation, the autumn rains (before ploughing) and the spring rains (for fruition) were absolutely essential for every Israelite farmer. Depending on where I am, reading these notes, I thank God for rain – or I pray earnestly for it.

This bright and sparkling picture of the land is framed in sombre colours. Whose blood does not run cold at the sight of the entire Egyptian army lying dead on the seashore (vs 3,4)?[1] When the ground opened up and swallowed Dathan, Abiram, their wives, children and little ones (v 6), all the Israelites fled.[2] Moses,

as it were, replays these incidents in front of his contemporary listeners' eyes (v 7). The warning against idolatry is repeated in verse 16. The very geography of the land, with the two peaks north and south of Samaria (vs 29,30; it seems clear that Moses' standpoint is *east* of the Jordan), symbolises the message of the chapter: the Israelites are faced with a choice – they should *choose* the blessing not the curse. This momentous command to choose is repeated later: 'Now choose life'.[3]

I read through the chapter again noticing, as so many times before, the verbs that depict the dimensions of this freedom. I ponder my freedom and my choices. If things are not ideal, it is common to look for someone, something to blame. Am I using to the full the freedom that God has given me to inherit his promises and do some good in the world?

Lord, help me to obey all the decrees and laws that you are setting before me today (v 32).

[1] See also Exod 14:30 [2] Num 16:25-34 [3] Deut 30:15,19

BIBLE IN A YEAR: Judges 13,14; Proverbs 7,8

WEDNESDAY 17 APRIL
Deuteronomy 12

God's Chosen Place

I read Psalm 84 or listen to Brahms' anthem, 'How Lovely is Thy Dwelling-Place', based on verse 1 of this psalm.

Horrible things went on 'on the high mountains … and under every spreading tree' (v 2), the worst of which is mentioned in verse 31. Aleksandr Solzhenitsyn, in his 1983 Templeton Address, summarised the dreadful things that had happened in the Western world in the twentieth century in four words, 'Men have forgotten God'. I review the six references in this chapter to 'the place the LORD your God will choose'. A particular place is not named and it is not said that there shall be only *one*. The key thing is that the Lord has his *name* (his well-defined, clearly revealed nature) and his *habitation* (his settled place among his people) there. Three times in this chapter, the Israelites are specifically commanded (!) to rejoice there (vs 7,12,18), a characteristic of the book of Deuteronomy.[1] Later, the Temple at Jerusalem became this special place;[2] later

still, biblical worship sprang away from a place to a Person, when the 'Word became flesh and made his dwelling among us'![3] The Lord is worshipped around the world in an amazing variety of buildings, but when these are blown up or swept away or forbidden or closed, the worship can still continue because we are worshipping a Person who has promised to be with us always.

There are some changes in the regulations for offering and eating, in preparation for the new circumstances in the Promised Land: for example, verse 20 is different from Leviticus 17:3 and 4. The Israelites are forbidden to eat the blood 'because the blood is the life' (v 23). I notice in particular how *inclusive* the celebrations and the worship of the Israelites are to be (vs 7,12,18,19), especially remembering the Levites, who had no physical inheritance.

I thank you, Jesus, that always, everywhere, in every circumstance I have access to the Father through you. I thank you for the people I meet in my place of worship.

[1] Deut 14:26; 16:11,14; 26:11; 27:7 [2] 1 Kings 8 [3] John 1:14; 4:20–26

BIBLE IN A YEAR: **Judges 15,16; Proverbs 9,10**

Deuteronomy 13

If...

Give me, Lord, an undivided heart to love you through everything.

This chapter is read in the synagogue in a barely audible voice. The three paragraphs all begin with the word 'If'. First, if a prophet or dreamer does signs or wonders, *even if they come true*, do not follow other gods. Second, if even a family member whom you love as your own soul tries to persuade you to go after other gods, you shall kill them. All Israel shall hear and fear. Third, if some troublemakers arise and draw away a whole city to follow other gods, after careful research and confirmation (v 14), subject the town and everything in it to the sacred ban. Don't let a single polluting thing in it stick to your fingers.

Clearly this chapter is not talking about trivial offences. It is not giving a raiders' charter to another town to accuse a rival and then loot it – because everything in the town is banned. What is described in this chapter is treason against the very foundation of Israel's existence, against the covenant, against the very first commandment. I remember the very drastic action that Elijah took against the prophets of Baal.[1]

It seems clear from the recurrence of idolatry, time and time again in the history of Israel, as we can read in the Old Testament, that these instructions must not have been followed. Missionaries (and those whom they have brought to know Jesus Christ) have often faced the difficult question of how to bring about *a separation* between the converts' new loyalty and their old religion. Boniface cut down Donar's oak; the demon gates of an Akha village in North Thailand may be broken down and burned. Abraham Lincoln was criticised for forgiving one of his opponent generals instead of destroying him; Lincoln's answer was, 'Do I not destroy my enemies by making them my friends?'

'Give me an undivided heart, that I may *fear your name*.'[2]

[1] 1 Kings 18:40 [2] Ps 86:11

BIBLE IN A YEAR: **Judges 17,18; Proverbs 11,12**

Be Different

I am not meant to be weird or bizarre or peculiar – but distinctive.

Israel is called God's firstborn son.[1] Here, for the first time in Deuteronomy, Israelites are reminded that they are 'children of the LORD' (v 1). Does my behaviour as a Christian stand out in any way in my society? Verse 1 refers to mourning customs of some sort – gashing, cutting, shaving. Chinese Christians have to act very carefully in not participating in some rituals of veneration of the spirits and yet showing true filial respect for the dead.

The food regulations which follow are similar to Leviticus 11, identifying animals on land, in the water and in the air. Cleanness and uncleanness apply not just to food but to other things as well, like skin diseases. Cleanness is an intermediate state between holiness and uncleanness. Israel is holy. Holiness and uncleanness cannot be mixed – and so the distinction between the different creatures appears to be that they must not be mixed; they must

belong properly to their kind. Perhaps the prohibition against cooking a young goat in its mother's milk (v 21) belongs to this area too – it is the basis of the Jewish practice of not mixing dairy and meat products.

Eating and hospitality are important in every culture. Paul reminded the Christians in Corinth to be careful about what they ate, for the sake of the 'brother or sister, for whom Christ died'.[2]

The rules about tithing are slightly different from those in Numbers 18: it seems there was a second, triennial tithe – a further opportunity to be generous! There is another reminder to remember the Levites. At the same time, verse 26 emphasises freedom of choice and rejoicing! The chapter ends under the bright sunshine of human hospitality and God's blessing. Generosity is a common theme in the Bible.[3]

Lord, make my home a place of conviviality and joy; a place to which people love to come, feeling God's presence here.

---

[1] Exod 4:22 [2] 1 Cor 8:11 [3] Eg Isa 58:10–12; Luke 6:38

Open Heart, Open Hands

I pray for generosity, especially towards those who are indebted to me in some way.

Two issues are dealt with briefly in this reading: cancelling debts and freeing servants. Both are to be done in a spirit of generosity and the words 'the LORD your God will bless you' (vs 4,6,10,18) are carried over from chapter 14 like a refrain.[1] The foreigner may be treated differently (v 3),[2] but this is not a permanent arrangement; it is just that intra-Israelite arrangements are like dealings within a family – your debtor is your brother. I ponder the apparent contradiction revealed in verses 4,7 and 11. There shouldn't really be any poor, indebted people in the land flowing with milk and honey. If the behaviour described here had been fully embedded, Israel would have been a wonderful, egalitarian society, but Moses is well aware of the people's history and so there *will* continue to be poor people in need of the generous release outlined here. Taking advantage of loopholes is a wicked sin. I review my own generosity and recollect the story of the widow in the Temple, putting in 'all she had to live on'.[3] I also remember Jesus' own words on the poor, reflecting verse 11.[4]

A servant is to be set free in the same spirit. Remember your history! You were once slaves in Egypt; consider all that God provided for you! So you are to provide bountifully for the servant who leaves you! How valuable his/her service has been. You are doubly blessed if your servant freely decides to stay with you! I feel in these texts the generosity of the law as it deals with these two difficult issues.

Jews have often been pictured in literature as rich, mean and stingy – but this is a libel. This chapter pictures a society in which people act *righteously*, with magnanimity.

I pray that I too may act with magnanimity, as a free and generous spirit in dealing with the debts and obligations of others to me.

[1] Deut 14:29 [2] Cf Deut 14:21 [3] Mark 12:44 [4] Mark 14:7

BIBLE IN A YEAR: **Judges 21; Proverbs 13,14**

Teamwork

I pray for my closest friends, that our bonds may grow even closer.

Placed between our readings in Deuteronomy 15 and 16, with all their conviviality and rejoicing, this psalm sits like a diamond in a ring. Israelis commonly dance when singing this psalm, repeating it again and again. The goodness and pleasure that comes from the unity of brothers and sisters is illustrated by two dramatic metaphors. I smell the fragrance of the first – the consecrating oil poured out over Aaron and his sons, over head, beard and collar; the specification of this oil is set out in Exodus.[1] Unity of believers is not an optional extra. It is a vital part of our faith and mission: 'By this everyone will know that you are my disciples, if you love one another.'[2]

The second metaphor is the dew of Hermon (in the far north) falling on Zion (in the south). I don't think this is a climatic miracle; it is probably a reference to abundant dew, like that of Hermon, falling (we know dew does not really fall) on the parched hills of Judea and especially Mount Zion. I pause to reflect on any experiences I have had or stories I have read of believers working together and thus bringing refreshment and encouragement and hope to whole communities. Often these events are the result of one person of prayer and courage taking an initiative for the sake of others – I pray that I may be such a person. The promise of this psalm is that *there* (in Jerusalem) God is going to bestow his blessing. It is a sad and tragic irony that, through David's dalliance in Jerusalem,[3] a whole sequence of events unfolded, bringing discord and death through his whole kingdom.

Are the words 'running down ... falling' (vs 2,3) a challenge, regarding the humility needed for energetic unity? Or a reminder that this wonderful gift comes down from God?

---

[1] Exod 30:23–25 [2] John 13:35 [3] 2 Sam 11

BIBLE IN A YEAR: **Ruth 1,2; Proverbs 15,16**

MONDAY 22 APRIL
Deuteronomy 15:19 – 16:17

Celebrations

I thank you, Lord, for the feasts and fasts of the Christian year, which are staging posts for our earthly pilgrimage.

This series of readings ends with another explosion of joy today in the three great annual Jewish festivals – *Pesach, Shavuot* and *Sukkot.* I notice, as I read, the characteristic themes that have been sounding all through these chapters: the place that God will choose, the inclusiveness, no mixing kinds, the generosity, the rejoicing, the sense of history. Passover is celebrated in memory of the greatest event in the Old Testament – the Exodus. Unleavened bread, the 'bread of affliction' (16:3), is a reminder of the trials and troubles surrounding that event. There is no daubing of the doorposts with blood, however, for there is now no threat to the firstborn. The Passover was eaten in haste, standing; but the Last Supper was eaten in the upper room, reclining, with long, meditative teaching.

Israel in Bible times was on the edge of a vast desert. Without the rains, nothing would grow. Every harvest was a miracle to be celebrated with abundant offerings; eight particular guests are specifically mentioned – a representation for everyone. The rain from heaven fell upon the just and the unjust – and all should give thanks. Is my church known for its generous hospitality in our community?

Tabernacles are also for everyone. There are special celebrations in the synagogue like the dancing of *Simchat Torah.* The joy of these festivals is not a private, guarded joy: it is social, communal, national. Somehow or other, the Jewish community has retained its capacity to celebrate and we hear an echo of Jesus' words in verse 15![1] The words 'law' and 'joy', not always associated together, are intimately interwoven, each resulting in and providing motivation for the other. If I live in a law-abiding society, I thank God.

'I have hidden your word in my heart that I might not sin against you.'[2]

[1] John 16:24 [2] Ps 119:11

BIBLE IN A YEAR: **Ruth 3,4; Psalm 45**

32

Jump into a new adventure this summer!

Can we count you in?

Volunteering with Scripture Union is more than just an adventure, it's life-changing!

Each year we host action-packed, faith-filled holidays and missions for hundreds of children, helping them create lasting memories while having the time of their lives! Could you take a break from the day job and volunteer with us?

FIND OUT MORE AND REGISTER TO VOLUNTEER: SU.ORG.UK/COUNTMEIN

✦ Scripture Union

Acts 17:1 – 21:26

NO MATTER WHAT IT COSTS

The book of Acts can be roughly divided into four parts. The first comprises chapters 1–7, covering the start of the Christian church in Jerusalem, where 'the Way'[1] was a sect of Judaism. The second part, chapters 8–15, documents the Christians who were leaving Jerusalem during the persecution after the martyrdom of Stephen, taking the gospel to Samaria and Antioch. This was followed by Paul's and Barnabas' first missionary journey and the Jerusalem Council. The third part is chapters 16–20, covering Paul's second and third missionary journeys, in which the gospel spread to Europe and Greece. The fourth is chapters 21–28, with Paul's arrest in Jerusalem and his journey to Rome for trial before the Roman Emperor. All this follows the key verse of Acts 1:8, 'But you will receive power when the Holy Spirit comes on you; and you will be my witnesses in Jerusalem, and in all Judea and Samaria, and to the ends of the earth'. The portion we are studying in this set of notes, chapters 17–21, comes in the third and fourth sections of Acts.

We must not forget that although Luke ends the book of Acts in Rome, that was not the end of Paul's ministry. He was later released and went on to Spain. Also, Acts is mainly about Peter's and Paul's ministry and does not relate the acts of the other apostles in other parts of the world – such as, according to tradition, Thomas' ministry in remotest India.

We will be looking at Paul's ministry to Greece and how he sets his face to doing God's will, irrespective of what it will cost. A good lesson for all of us.

Peter S C Pothan

FOR FURTHER READING

John Stott, *The Message of Acts*, BST Series, second revised edition, IVP, 1991
William Barclay, *The Acts of the Apostles*, Daily Study Bible Series, revised edition, Westminster John Knox Press, 1976
Craig S Keener, *The IVP Bible Background Commentary: New Testament*, second edition, IVP USA, 2014

[1] Eg Acts 9:2; 24:14,22

Turmoil in Thessalonica

Prepare for your journey in Acts by asking God to open your heart and give you courage to confess your faith.

In Acts 16, Luke related Paul's vision of a man begging him to come to Macedonia. Paul and his companions concluded that God had called them to preach the gospel there: thus started the Greek (and European) mission.

They crossed the sea to Philippi where, in spite of having suffered and been insulted, Paul and Silas received strength from God to preach the gospel in Thessalonica, the capital of Macedonia located 75 miles southwest of Philippi. Thessalonica was a well-connected town, the residence of the provincial governor and a centre of business and commerce. We can see Paul's missional strategy – to cover the major cities and trust that from there the gospel will spread out, as it did from Ephesus to Colossae, Laodicea and other places.[1] We too need a clear strategy in our mission.

Paul stayed in Thessalonica for nearly a month and, as usual, started his ministry in the synagogue, where he reasoned with the worshippers about Jesus. He explained that Jesus had to suffer and rise from the dead, identifying him with the Christ of Scripture. Luke records a divided response to Paul's ministry. Some Jews were persuaded and joined Paul and Silas, perhaps in a house group, but the greatest response was from the Gentiles (v 4b). Among them were Aristarchus and Secundus, who later became Paul's fellow travellers;[2] Aristarchus also was his fellow prisoner.[3]

The unbelieving Jews rounded up some bad characters, formed a mob and started a riot in the city. They rushed to Jason's house in search of Paul and Silas, to bring them out to the crowd. When they did not find them, their host Jason was held responsible for their actions and was required to post bail. If Paul had been found, he would not have been so lucky.

Pray for those across the world who are suffering for spreading the gospel.

---

[1] John Stott, *The Message of Acts*, BST Series, second revised edition, IVP, 1991, p270 [2] Acts 20:4 [3] Acts 27:2; Col 4:10

BIBLE IN A YEAR: **1 Samuel 1–3; Proverbs 17,18**

Acts 17:10–15

Response at Berea

**Ask God to help you to listen to his Word and to hear his call on
your life.**

Paul and Silas were sent forty miles to Berea under the cover of darkness, to ensure that no further public disturbance began. Again they went first to the Jewish synagogue to preach, where many Jews and Greeks believed. However, as in Thessalonica, the response was divided.

William Barclay reminds us how important Thessalonica was.[1] The great Roman road from the Adriatic Sea to the Middle East was called the Egnatian Way and the main street of Thessalonica was actually part of that road. If Christianity was firmly rooted in Thessalonica, it could spread both east and west along that road, a highway for the kingdom of God. Considering all this, Luke chronicles these missions with surprising brevity, drawing our attention to the way the Scriptures were preached and heard. In Thessalonica Paul 'reasoned', 'explained', 'proved', 'proclaimed' and 'persuaded' (see vs 2–4), whereas in Berea the Jews eagerly 'received' the message and diligently 'examined' the Scriptures (v 11). Paul's arguments and his hearers' studies went hand in hand:[2] sound practice!

There are many false doctrines today and we need to check with the Word of God to see if the teachings we hear are biblical. When I decided to do my BD, I joined a college that was theologically very liberal. I decided to explore whether my evangelical faith was robust and so I applied my scientific training in mathematics and physics to my theological studies. I discovered that the Bible was accurate and trustworthy, but the particular brand of theology I was taught was often based on speculation. I came out believing more strongly than ever. I have continued to do this all my life. I encourage you to explore the Bible like this, questioning doctrines such as the prosperity gospel.

**Check everything you hear preached against the Scriptures and pray that the
Holy Spirit will lead you into all truth.**

---

[1] William Barclay, *The Acts of the Apostles*, Daily Study Bible Series, revised, Westminster John Knox, 1976, p127 [2] John Stott, 1991, p274,275

BIBLE IN A YEAR: **1 Samuel 4–6; Proverbs 19,20**

Paul in Athens

As you read this story today, ask God to prepare you to speak boldly of your faith.

Entering Athens alone, Paul went around the city like a tourist. The streets were lined with statues of men and gods, and pillars mounted with heads of Hermes: the evidence of Athenian piety. Paul began to preach daily in the marketplace, on Jesus and the resurrection. This confused many Greeks as they thought he was teaching about foreign gods.

They invited him to the Areopagus to share with the intellectuals. Here Paul gives his first recorded apologetic sermon. After praising them for their religiosity, he points out that there is only one God, the Lord of heaven and earth, who does not live in temples made by humans. He created all people and marked out their times and places (v 26). The aim is that they should worship God everywhere.

This important claim teaches us that God has a plan and place for our lives. God made me an Indian and his plan is for me to minister in this country. When I worked in a theological college, I was upset to see so many young men trying to get to the 'Promised Land' of the US instead of ministering in India. Of course, if God calls you to minister elsewhere you should go, but not for the goal of financial success. God uses believing Christians in every walk of life, not just in so-called 'full-time' service. As I read the *Management Devotional*[1] daily, I am overjoyed to see the many believers in Indian industry making a mark by their Christian principles.

Scholars are divided on the apparently poor results of Paul's sermon, but Luke observes that Dionysius, a leader in the Areopagus, is converted and many others including many prominent women like Damaris.

Ask God to show you new ways to reach unbelievers wherever you encounter people open to him.

[1] *Management Devotional*, published by Christian Manager, has daily devotions written by lay people in the faith for working professionals

BIBLE IN A YEAR: **1 Samuel 7–9; Proverbs 21,22**

Acts 18:1–11

Hearing God's Voice

Open your ears and heart now to hear from God's Word.

Paul's next stop, Corinth, was the political and economic centre of Greece. It was also on the way to Rome. Paul stayed in Corinth for about 18 months (a long stay) and was thus able to draw the believers into a more established and mature network. Ministries can be short or long and will achieve different results. Aquila and Priscilla, Paul's hosts, were, like him, tent makers. Paul could tell the Corinthian church that he worked for his living and was not a financial burden.[1] Tent making is important – you work to meet your needs and preach in your spare time. This was one way in which the college student ministry grew in India, as graduates became tent-maker ministers.

The arrival of Silas and Timothy enabled Paul to give himself to the ministry more fully (v 5). Was it this that caused the Jews to turn against him? Paul decided to focus on the Gentiles[2] and a house church seems to have started in the home of Titius Justus. The synagogue ruler, Crispus, and his wider household, all came to faith. We may think our witness goes unheard, but God can use our efforts to change hearts. God spoke to Paul and encouraged him to go on preaching, in spite of the challenges, because the many believers in Corinth would protect him (vs 9,10). We too need to be guided by God every step of the way. He will guide us through our daily devotions, speakers, sermons and Christian books – and through the 'still small voice'.[3]

I have heard God's voice several times in guidance. In 1971, during the Union of Evangelical Students of India's Missionary Conference, God told me in an audible voice, 'This is my place for you in my ministry', thus leading me into the literature ministry.

Pray for God's clear guidance in your life and ministry; may God help you to hear his voice.

---

[1] 2 Cor 11:9   [2] See also Acts 13:46   [3] 1 Kings 19:12, ASV

BIBLE IN A YEAR: **1 Samuel 10,11; Psalms 46,47**

Paul before Gallio

Ask God to give you hope and opportunity to share the gospel. Pray that doors which seem closed might open for mission.

Once again, the spread of the gospel receives assistance from a surprising source. Gallio was the Roman proconsul (governor) of Achaia and gave judgements publicly on breaches of the Roman law.

We can thus see another side of Roman justice, so different from what happened in Philippi.[1] The Jews must have suggested that Paul had broken Roman law, because religious disputes were not under his jurisdiction.[2] Gallio, however, considered the Jews to be troublemakers and refused to listen to them. Even when they turned on their own leader (Sosthenes must have replaced Crispus), he paid no attention, so the Jewish plot backfired. Gallio's fair-mindedness allowed Paul's mission to continue.

Paul might have felt nervous after this experience but, in spite of his narrow escape, he did not leave immediately but stayed in Corinth to continue establishing the faith. This cosmopolitan trading centre was important for mission, so this extra time was well spent. It can be easy to move on or to quit when things get tough, but that is not always God's call.

Paul did not want deliberately to alienate his Jewish brothers and sisters. Perhaps that is why he cut his hair – to keep a religious vow – although we do not know why Luke mentions it. He then spends time in the synagogue at Ephesus and, because he is well received, he determines to come back if he can to help the believers. In all this we can see God's promise to Paul 'no one is going to … harm you' (v 10) in action. Roman law here protected Paul and enabled the spread of the gospel. Unfortunately, there are many places today where Christians cannot count on the law to protect and enable their ministry.

Pray for those who are facing persecution today for the sake of Jesus.

[1] Acts 16:16–40 [2] See Pilate's initial response to the charges against Jesus, John 18:31

BIBLE IN A YEAR: 1 Samuel 12,13; Proverbs 23,24

SUNDAY 28 APRIL
Psalm 134

Pinnacle of Praise

Let us praise the Lord morning and night.

There are many ways of going on a pilgrimage. We can take a long walk, cutting back our daily needs so that we can focus on God. We might instead do a pilgrimage of the heart and set ourselves tasks for each day to remind us of God. We might use a labyrinth to help us to focus on prayer. The psalter contains 15 psalms of ascent, of which the very short Psalm 134 is the last. These psalms were used as pilgrimage steps. Psalm 134 is the climax of the journey towards God – a shout of praise.

This psalm contains a call to worship, presenting the greatness of God (vs 1,2), and invites us to experience the joy of his blessings (v 3). It was probably a priestly liturgy.[1] God is the Maker of heaven and earth but he is also approachable for us humans, for our praise and worship. The psalm was probably used at night (v 1) and might have been used during the Feast of Tabernacles.[2]

What is beyond doubt is the call to praise the Lord. Yet it also opens up the idea that this praise and blessing goes in two directions: God receives our praise; we are blessed by the Lord. Being praiseful brings its own blessing. To remember that we are eternally beloved, even in the hardest times, is a way of praising God even when we cannot feel the joy. His praiseworthiness is a fact; his blessing of us is a fact. There are times when we run out of words of our own or we cannot find anything to say to God because we are sad. At those times, let us read Psalm 134 and remember that we are blessed and he is the blesser. Always and for ever. Hallelujah.

Read this psalm slowly and receive God's blessing. Write it out and read it every day this week, praising the Lord with these ancient words.

[1] Leslie C Allen, *Psalms 101-150*, Word Biblical Commentary, Word Books, 1983, p220 [2] Allen, 1983, p218

BIBLE IN A YEAR: **1 Samuel 14,15; Proverbs 25,26**

Acts 18:23–28

Apollos' Enlightenment

We are called to share our faith with others. Ask God to make you both sensitive and bold.

The Word of God has power to convict and convert. We remember the Ethiopian eunuch,[1] who became curious about the Messiah from reading the book of Isaiah. Here we read of Apollos, whose heart had been opened by the Word, though we are not told how he became a believer. There must have been many preachers and evangelists who had scattered out from Jerusalem, although Acts focuses on Paul, Peter and a few others. We can thank God for faithful yet unsung missionaries and pray for anyone we know who has served in that way.

This passage shows us the importance of nurturing believers in the study of the Scriptures. When they arrived at Ephesus, Aquila and Priscilla set up their tent-making business (see v 3) and worked there for some years. They hosted a church in their home.[2] Because Paul had been received well by the synagogue leader, Crispus, that church had grown (v 8). Paul trusted Priscilla and Aquila to nurture this church and disciple the new Christians. We see God's timing in bringing Apollos, an evangelist, through the synagogue into contact with the Christians who could deepen his knowledge of Jesus.

Later Apollos went to Achaia where he preached powerfully and refuted the Jews in public debates. He apparently focused his ministry in Achaia, where unfortunately a division developed between those who followed him and those who followed Paul.[3] Paul, however, perceived their relationship as co-workers. Paul planted, Apollos watered and God gave the increase.[4] We all have different roles in ministry according to our gifts. There is no need for jealousy. Let us do what calls God us to do.

Let us encourage and disciple new believers so they become worthy workers for God and be content with our callings.

---

[1] Acts 8:26–40 [2] 1 Cor 16:19 [3] See 1 Cor 1:12 [4] See 1 Cor 3:5,6

BIBLE IN A YEAR: **1 Samuel 16,17; Psalm 48**

Acts 19:1–12

Power in Ephesus

'Be still, for the power of the Lord is moving in this place.'[1]

It can be hard to know when to move on from a ministry and when to stay put. 'Shake the dust off your feet' is a gospel strategy sometimes and we must discern when it is right. Having stayed for a long time in Corinth and having had the opportunity to develop and mature the converts there, Paul now stays two years in Ephesus, another key urban centre with connections that served the spread of the good news.

Paul's first recorded work there is to pray for the Spirit to fill the disciples in Ephesus – and this was the beginning of a power-filled time of witness and ministry. Twelve men received the Spirit and they formed the nucleus of the Ephesian church. Paul's synagogue preaching led again to a mixed response towards the message of Jesus. He decided to move out of the synagogue with the disciples and began teaching in a lecture hall instead.

We may have explored our own moves out of church buildings and into less obviously religious premises, in order to develop new missional movements and wider contacts in our communities.

The church in Ephesus was well established, widely connected and strategic. It seemed to be a centre for training and developing new Christians. It was also a place of powerful acts of the Holy Spirit. Paul performed miraculous healings (vs 11,12) and these must have helped the growth of the church.

We can see many different ways in which the Holy Spirit was active in Paul's ministry: empowered preaching, discernment and miracles. We should seek also to see the Spirit's activity in our own ministry, not only in the church but in our workplaces.

Where have you seen God's greatness and the moving of the Holy Spirit in your own life and in the wider world? Thank and praise him for these experiences.

[1] David J Evans, b1957, 'Be still, for the presence of the Lord'

BIBLE IN A YEAR: **1 Samuel 18,19; Proverbs 27,28**

The Inadequacy of Magic

'Spirit of holiness, wisdom and faithfulness, / wind of the Lord, blowing strongly and free ... Spirit of God, bring your fullness to me!' [1]

In the Western world, many people would say they don't really believe in magic or the supernatural – but they are still fascinated by it. As Christian adherence declines in the West, there is an interest in alternative spiritualities that are nothing to do with the Holy Spirit. In many other parts of the globe, such spirituality is deeply embedded in the culture and rituals of the local community. We are all wise if we are alert to the kind of power we might be calling upon.

We noted yesterday how the Holy Spirit worked through Paul in Ephesus. Of course, when God works, the devil is also active in producing spurious miracles. Some of the itinerant Jewish exorcists tried using the name of Jesus over those who had evil spirits. The seven sons of Sceva the priest were doing this, but their misguided efforts backfired. It is clear that they had no personal faith in Jesus, except perhaps some knowledge of the power associated with his name. They hoped to capitalise on the use of Jesus' name but failed.

The result in superstition-ridden Ephesus is powerful. Luke explains that when this event became known to the Jews and Greeks there, they were seized with fear and honoured the name of Jesus, burning their valuable magic scrolls.

This turning towards Jesus and reliance on the Holy Spirit lent divine power to the work in Ephesus, which was a centre for magic in the Roman world. Are there things in our lives that we should relinquish? Things that hold us and fascinate us more than they should, or maybe things we have just never thought about? Let us burn our scrolls (cf v 19) and commit ourselves to the Lord and his work.

Pray for the guidance and power of the Holy Spirit to give us life in Jesus.

---

[1] Christopher Idle, b1938, 'Spirit of Holiness'

BIBLE IN A YEAR: **1 Samuel 20–22; Proverbs 29,30**

Acts 19:23–41

Law on Our Side

Pray for a pure heart, first to see the truth and then to be brave enough to pursue it.

Have you ever had to sacrifice profit or other material benefit for the sake of Christ? There are many things that can become idols for us. We can very easily put our well-being before our commitment. An idol takes the place in our hearts that God should take, but sometimes this is very subtle and hard to see.

Luke shows us several times how the power of God can overcome all other powers. He tells us of a riot taking place in Ephesus, triggered by this question of idolatry. As Christianity grew and challenged local superstition, the business of the silversmiths who made idols of the goddess Artemis of Ephesus was suffering. Paul was preaching that gods made by men were not gods at all – and so the idol-makers were going bankrupt. Demetrius, a local smith, instigated the riot and it could have turned out very badly for Paul. However, the disciples and the 'officials of the province' (v 31) persuaded Paul not to enter the theatre and address the crowd. Paul clearly had friends in high places and this was significant.

The town clerk seems to have calmed the rioters down. He reminds Demetrius that there is a proper legal process if he wants to make a complaint. He does not need to resort to civil disobedience. Once again we see that Roman law can be used by God to help the gospel to spread.

Luke discusses this riot at length, after describing many miracles taking place under Paul's ministry. The mission in Ephesus adds a new dimension to our understanding of God: God cannot be conceived in terms of man-made idols. In India, as in other places, Christian work can be opposed for similar reasons.

How is the gospel being challenged where you live? Are those around you aware of it? Pray for those who preach the Word.

BIBLE IN A YEAR: **1 Samuel 23,24; Proverbs 31**

Paul in Troas

'O worship the King, all-glorious above'.[1]

After the Ephesian riot, Paul left for Macedonia, where he had sent Timothy and Erastus, his helpers, in advance.[2] Paul's journeys are often quite convoluted and it is likely that he chose his route so that he could visit and encourage churches that he knew while he was travelling. Evangelism and mission cannot be separated from pastoral care and discipleship. Paul was about to sail to Syria but, because of a plot against him, he decided to go back through Macedonia, accompanied by many co-workers, including Luke. Paul believed in team ministry and never worked alone. He used the companionship, gifts and connections of others – a good example for us today.

Luke explains that the others went on ahead to Troas while Paul stayed for the Feast of the Unleavened Bread and followed later. Troas is another strategic centre for gospel connections. The church here seems well established, since Luke describes a worship service. This is the early church being the church: we may recognise elements in our own worship!

Luke's description of Paul's long and winding journey to Jerusalem resembles his description of Jesus' journey to Jerusalem. Paul travels with his disciples, experiences challenges from the Jewish leaders and is determined to get there for Pentecost. Luke may be emphasising the nature of discipleship for those who follow Jesus. He also tells us about Eutychus, the young man who falls from the window while Paul preaches and is discovered to be dead (Luke of course is a doctor). Paul effects a miracle by laying hands on the young man[3] and Eutychus recovers. Paul allows the power of God to flow through him. Then he leaves for the next bit of his journey.

Reflect on the way our worship is connected with those early Christians and give thanks that Jesus Christ is the same yesterday, today and for ever. Worship him now.

[1] Robert Grant, 1779–1838 [2] See Acts 19:22 [3] Like Elijah in 1 Kings 17

BIBLE IN A YEAR: **1 Samuel 25,26; Psalm 49**

Acts 20:17–38

Paul's Farewell Speech

What would you say to the people you love if you knew you would never see them again? Reflect on what is most important to you about the relationship.

I wonder whether Luke took notes during this speech, or whether he just had a very good memory! For he was almost certainly with the elders of the Ephesian church when Paul made this heartfelt address to them – Luke uses 'we' in verse 13 and then in 21:1. Clearly this speech made a great impact on everyone present – they all wept (v 37).

Paul is now on his way back to Jerusalem, to be there at Pentecost, so he summons the elders of the Ephesian church, with which he had been so involved, to meet him in Miletus. Paul appeals to their knowledge of him and his ministry to defend his integrity, knowing that he may meet persecution ahead in Jerusalem (vs 22–24). Yet he is 'compelled by the Spirit' to go and he puts the goal of preaching Jesus ahead of any personal threat or discomfort. What a challenge this is to us as we go about our daily lives!

Paul also gives advice to the church leaders, because he knows he will not see them again (v 25). He warns them to stay true, to 'watch' (v 28) their own spiritual lives and to be watchful towards those who will accuse and challenge them. In particular, pastors must never be susceptible to personal gain at the expense of the flock. Whether or not we are in leadership, we need to remain accountable to God and we do this by being accountable to others in Christ. This is of particular importance in the formation of new ministers and leaders.

Paul's clear understanding that he would never return to them was hard for them to bear. This apostle, who was full of passion and learning and could be so firm, was also dearly beloved.

Think about the leaders in your own church and give thanks for those who have helped you on your Christian journey.

BIBLE IN A YEAR: **1 Samuel 27,28; 1 Corinthians 1**

Our God is Greater

'My God, how wonderful thou art, / thy majesty how bright'.[1]

Many of our worship songs in church use phrases taken straight from the Bible, the psalms being a favourite source because of the beauty of their poetry and images. Psalm 135 is an ancient hymn of praise that was probably used during one of the feasts, with a post-exilic congregation gathered to praise God. Interesting for us is the way this psalm uses bits of other psalms and texts in the Old Testament. Leslie Allen says that if we read carefully we will find ourselves 'assailed by a conglomeration of snatches of other parts of the OT'.[2] What a beautiful composition emerges! This is real poetry, with a beautiful shape and structure, and real praise, remembering God's past deliverance and his future promise to his people, and naming his power over all creation.

The writer asks us to see God as 'our' God (v 2) – the God who has chosen to be in covenant relationship with his people (v 4). The psalmist then gives some reasons to praise the Lord. Beautiful images assault us as we read of his creative power in making clouds rise and bringing the wind from the storehouse, followed by memories of powerful interventions. As a people that has been imprisoned and released, exiled and restored, there is plenty of awareness of the religions of the other nations that surround and tempt Israel to be faithless. The psalmist dismisses these other gods (v 5) and idols (vs 15–18) as powerless, hopeless and pointless in the light of the glory of the Lord.

I have often seen the worship of idols and they are simply statues made and carried around by people. They have no power. Thank God, we worship a Lord who is unchanging and is daily with us, and carries us – not the reverse. Our God is greater. Praise the Lord.

How much more have we to thank God and praise him for? Count your blessings and praise him.

---

[1] FW Faber, 1814–63 [2] Leslie C Allen, *Psalms 101–150*, Word Biblical Commentary, Word Books, 1983, p224

BIBLE IN A YEAR: **1 Samuel 29–31; 1 Corinthians 2**

Acts 21:1–16

Agabus' Prophecy

Ask the Holy Spirit to lay clearly before you what God is saying to you from today's reading.

It is hard to part from people we love. Paul here undergoes a difficult parting from the churches he loves: 'After we had torn ourselves away' (vs 1,5,6).

We continue with Paul's journey to Jerusalem. William Barclay notes, 'The narrative is speeding up and there is an atmosphere of approaching storm as Paul comes nearer Jerusalem. There is the sheer determination of Paul to go on no matter what lies ahead.'[1] Paul took a complicated route to Jerusalem involving three ships – why did he not go to Antioch and report to the church as usual and then go on? Because he wanted to reach Jerusalem 'if possible, by the day of Pentecost'.[2]

Luke describes multiple warnings to Paul about going to Jerusalem, not least the graphic prophecy of Agabus in which he ties his feet and hands to show how Paul will be bound. There are echoes of other biblical stories – the prophetic acting of the Old Testament, for example, and Jesus' warning to Peter.[3] We might wonder why the Holy Spirit, who 'compelled' Paul to go to Jerusalem,[4] also seems to warn him of what awaits him there. Probably the Spirit gave prophetic foresight to the believers, who passed the warning on to Paul – adding their own human opinions to the message.

What is your reaction if being faithful also means putting yourself at risk in some way? This requires discernment and we should always consult others if possible. Missionaries throughout the centuries often went ahead in spite of danger. Polycarp was burned at the stake and said, 'How can I deny Christ, he has done me no harm?' These words were repeated by Thomas Cranmer, who designed the Anglican Prayer Book, as he was burned at the command of Queen Mary in Broad Street in Oxford.

Pray that you will be a brave witness if you are ever tested.

---

[1] William Barclay, *The Acts of the Apostles*, Westminster John Knox, 1976, p153,154
[2] Acts 20:16 [3] John 21:18,19 [4] Acts:20:22

BIBLE IN A YEAR: **2 Samuel 1,2; Psalm 50**

Paul in Jerusalem

Sometimes it can be hard to accept the views of others. Ask God to speak his gracious acceptance into your heart today, if this is your situation.

Differences between Christians can be challenging. Sometimes alternative views are held and defended very fiercely. There can be a lot of emotion, because everyone is highly invested in living a godly life and will want to do his or her best for God. Here, Paul and his team may have anxieties about their reception by the Christians at Jerusalem, where they have arrived after their long, difficult and possibly dangerous journey. Luke reports that they are greeted 'warmly' (v 17). After a night's sleep, the missionaries go to see James, who still leads the Jerusalem church. They may have been anticipating a tense and unsettling meeting. Luke has recorded earlier the significant differences of opinion between those involved in the Jewish and the Gentile Christian missions.[1]

A wonderful testimony to the grace and love that is possible through Christ became apparent. Paul told James and the elders stories of the many Gentile conversions he had seen – and the brothers in Jerusalem were full of praise to God for the spread of the gospel. With a similar generosity of spirit, Paul agreed to undergo a Jewish ritual to reassure the Jerusalem brethren that he was not abandoning or rejecting their customs. This was an example of loving acceptance of one another's differences in Christ. Before many more years, all the Christians in Jerusalem would be persecuted for their faith, irrespective of their Jewish or Gentile pedigrees.

It is important to proclaim the faith, to plant churches and to teach and train disciples. It is also important to embrace the gentleness of Christ towards one another. Paul's missionary journeys were incredible human achievements, but his heart was shaped by generosity and kindness. He was truly a captive of Christ.

Pray for God's grace to fill your own heart with love and may this be part of your witness for Christ.

[1] Acts 15

BIBLE IN A YEAR: **2 Samuel 3–5; 1 Corinthians 3**

Scripture Union

Know someone moving up to secondary school?

It's Your Move helps children take the giant step from primary to secondary school, with stories and tips from recent leavers, as well as teachers and schools workers. These great little books also feature reflections on how the Christian faith can help at this daunting time, making a great gift for children in Year 6.

IT'S YOUR MOVE
YOUR SECONDARY SCHOOL SURVIVAL GUIDE

- A survival guide, survival journal and survival stories to help children adapt to a new school.

- Top tips and stories from children who have already made the move, with additional content available online.

- Advice and space to reflect alongside Bible references.

- Over 2 million children already helped settle into their new school through this series.

FREEDOM IN CHRIST

Over the next two weeks we will be digging into Paul's letter to the fledgling church in Galatia, which is one of the earliest pieces of Christian writing. We will encounter Paul's deep concern for the Galatian churches he had founded on his first missionary journey. After he left them, false teachers had infiltrated the community of Gentile converts and were promoting a distorted version of the gospel. These teachers, known as Judaisers, claimed that Gentile believers must first become Jewish by following the Jewish law so that they would be saved. Be prepared for the strong language used by Paul as he expresses his frustration with the Galatians who had succumbed to this pressure and were conforming to Jewish legalism.

Central to Paul's thread throughout the letter is the declaration that our standing with God is not based on anything we might do, but purely on what Christ has done. He consistently points to the hope that we have in Christ and the futility of looking for our hope anywhere else. As we weave our way through this letter, we'll encounter moments when Paul's frustration hits some lofty peaks. He refers to those whom he clearly held in great affection as 'foolish', questioning who has 'bewitched' them (3:1). His holy indignation is more fiercely targeted at the bewitchers, as he uses shocking images to demonstrate the seriousness of the situation.

Despite the strong language used, this letter is ultimately a message of hope. Each day when we consider Paul's words, ask God to remind you of the power of the gospel and the freedom we have in Christ. Our context will be different to that of Galatia (in what is now Turkey) in around AD 50, but the compulsion to conform to the world's standards remains. May God grant each of us the wisdom and courage to allow these ancient words to be applied to our lives as disciples and also to the churches and communities in which we live.

Jonny Libby

Astonishing Indignation

Father, as we begin this letter, give us ears to hear what the Spirit is saying.

Paul begins this letter differently from others he wrote. He extends the same 'grace and peace' as he does elsewhere, but begins here in the context of rescue from the present evil age (v 4). The tone is very different from the thankful remembrance extended to the Philippians[1] – and Paul gets quickly to the point. Many commentators refer to verse 6 as the start of the 'rebuke' section of the letter – which continues until we reach 4:11. So, fasten up tight for the ride!

Paul's astonishment is not centred on the Galatians rejecting the gospel message, but rather their rejection of Christ. He is clearly frustrated with the new believers in Galatia, but this frustration is directed towards those who had been deceiving them. Paul uses provocative language to describe their deception, and this anger and language will intensify later in the letter. The 'some people' Paul refers to in verse 7 are those who were teaching the Galatian converts that accepting the gospel message proclaimed by Paul was not enough and that to be fully Christian they must first become Jews and adopt Jewish religious practices. Paul curses these Judaisers and will continue to do so throughout the letter.

You may appreciate Paul's indignation here, but there is a need for introspection. What have we, ourselves, subtly added to the gospel as a prerequisite for God's acceptance? Are you attending church often enough? Do you pray daily? Dare I say, are you keeping up with your daily Bible study notes or, like me, often catching up? Of themselves, all these are valuable, but we should engage in them as a consequence of the faith we hold and not as a form of Christian loyalty card to earn grace. May we never allow our study to become a mere quest for knowledge, but rather a means to know God better.

What may you have added to the gospel? Rejoice that your hope is in the finished work of Christ.

[1] Phil 1:3

BIBLE IN A YEAR: **2 Samuel 6,7; 1 Corinthians 4**

Galatians 1:11–24

Persecutor to Preacher

'My hope is built on nothing less / than Jesus' blood and righteousness'.[1]

In defending his ministry, Paul describes himself before his conversion, then his encounter with Christ, and his actions after God had called him. In the description of his former life, Paul himself is the subject of the verbs: 'I persecuted ... [I] tried to destroy ... I was advancing in Judaism ... [I] was extremely zealous' (vs 13,14). Yet, when defining his conversion and subsequent calling, God becomes the subject of the verbs: 'God, who set me apart ... called me ... [revealed] his Son in me' (vs 15,16). For those who are in Christ, this is your story too. To the Galatians, Paul's appeal is to rely fully on the completed work of Christ.

The conclusion of Paul's conversion account centres on the source of his revelation. I recall hearing someone describe revelation as 'something you know only because God told you'. Paul's argument is that, in turning away from the gospel that he had declared, the Galatians are actually turning away from God, since the gospel revealed to Paul came to him directly from God. It could be implied that this received teaching from God came to Paul when he was in Arabia for three years (vs 17,18). This information regarding the timeline of Paul's ministry is easily overlooked. We might assume, from reading Acts 9:25 and 26, that Paul went immediately to Jerusalem.

The enthusiastic response of the Judean churches (v 24) to Paul's ministry is a clear rebuke of the subversion of the Galatian churches by the Judaisers. Not only that, but I also believe that Paul mentions this response to avert any suspicion of a conflict between the gospel to Jews and that to the Gentiles (see tomorrow's note). How the church deals with difference is as important now as it was then. May God give us the wisdom to hold independence and convergence in balance.

Take a few minutes to consider who you were before Christ saved you. Rejoice in whose you are now.

---

[1] Edward Mote, 1797–1874

Galatians 2:1–10

Resilience in the Truth

Father, enable us to be enthralled once again by the wonder of the gospel.

'The bane of Paul's life and ministry was the insidious activity of false teachers.'[1] After 14 years away from Jerusalem (with the exception of a 15-day visit),[2] Paul now returns there. The key issue at hand is the suggestion that he was teaching a different message from Peter. To counter this allegation, he details those who accompanied him on his second trip to Jerusalem – Barnabas the Jew, along with Titus the uncircumcised Greek. The issue at hand regards compulsion. I am confident that Paul would have no issue with a Gentile convert adopting some of the Jewish practices. However, we'll see vehement arguments against those who were advocating the necessity of such practices to attain real Christian status.

This meeting in Jerusalem would no doubt have been a tense occasion, as the apostles in Jerusalem were presented with Paul's Gentile companion. I'm sure many of you have been in challenging meetings. Imagine being present at the meeting of Paul, James, John and Peter. From Paul's description it seems to have been a meeting full of grace.

The positive outcome of the discussion was that the right hand of fellowship was given. They recognised, however, that, although they had been entrusted with the same gospel, they had been allocated different spheres in which to preach it. Having established that the style and emphasis of Paul's ministry was distinctive and for a particular audience, Paul lets us in on the action point that emerged from the meeting. After agreeing the ministries to which each was called, all that was asked of Paul was a remembrance of the poor. Oh that more tense church meetings would conclude with the rallying call to serve the least and the lost!

What does the Lord require of you today? Take a moment to read Micah 6:8.

---

[1] John Stott, *Only One Way*, IVP, 1974, p39 [2] Gal 1:18

BIBLE IN A YEAR: **2 Samuel 11,12; Psalm 51**

Living by Faith Alone

Father, give us eyes to look on ourselves today in the same way as you view us.

These are some of the most awkward verses of Scripture. Paul's public rebuke of Peter, whom he'd just referred to as a pillar of the church (v 9) seems quite remarkable. The specific issue under debate here is what, and with whom, one eats. Paul here accuses Peter of hypocrisy, seemingly leading to Galatia having both Gentile and kosher groups of believers. This seems all the more remarkable given the vision Peter had received from God on this very issue.[1]

However, the bigger issue Paul is addressing is 'the truth of the gospel' (v 14). Paul uses this phrase for the second time here in a few verses (see also v 5) and it is a thread that we'll see throughout the letter. Paul wants the reader to know beyond any doubt that one is accepted by God (justified) by the sheer grace of God alone, through faith alone. This is the primary issue of deep concern to Paul and

should be for us today. I heard someone recently say that they were exhausted from the pressure to impress others. Paul would urge us to die to such expectations of ourselves and find our value in Christ.

Paul's exposition (vs 15,16) moves to argument (vs 17–21), in which he lays out the fallacy of our attempts to please God, in contrast to the wonder of finding our identity in Christ. Paul describes this in terms of a death and a resurrection and how, astonishingly, we share in the redemptive acts of Christ. In contrast to those who had insisted on strict observance of the law, Paul contends that the new creation is now dead to its demands. As Paul writes to the Colossians, Christ has nailed the law, which was contrary to us, to his cross.[2] This is wonderful news for us all.

Take a moment to consider anything that you need to hand once again to Christ and allow him to nail it to his cross.

[1] Acts 10,11 [2] Col 2:14,15; Gal 3:13; Eph 2:14–16

BIBLE IN A YEAR: **2 Samuel 13,14; 1 Corinthians 6**

Psalm 136

The Power of Remembering

Father, incline our minds towards you today and accept our grateful thanks.

Psalm 136 is unique among the psalms in that it employs a repeated refrain, 'His love endures for ever'. I wonder if, as you read, you took time to take a breath and read this refrain each time? If, like me, you often succumb to the tendency to skim over repeated phrases, I invite you to find time at some point today to pause, read again and take a moment to consider each verse and breathe in the enduring love of God.

The psalmist gives us a wonderful framework for expressing thanksgiving. Initially, praise is focused on what is visible in the present; then it proceeds to dwell on God's faithfulness in the past. We are reminded here that every good and perfect gift comes from him and, despite our own failing, the love of God still endures for ever. God's faithfulness in the past and the assurance of his current presence give us all such a firm foundation and hope for what lies ahead.

This may sound an odd question, but I wonder if you've ever written a psalm? Take a moment to look at the beauty of this day. The sun rose this morning and will set tonight – only God can cause astonishing things like that to happen. You may face challenging circumstances today, so take time to consider his faithfulness in the past. How about using the refrain of this psalm to sandwich each reason you have to give praise? I've just done this myself and stuck my words of thankfulness into my Bible as Psalm 151. I know that we are commanded not to add or subtract from the Scriptures,[1] but I think God will be OK with this.

Paul urges us to 'give thanks in all circumstances'.[2] Take a moment to reflect on your circumstances and rejoice that your Saviour is right there with you.

---

[1] Deut 4:2 [2] 1 Thess 5:18

BIBLE IN A YEAR: **2 Samuel 15,16; 1 Corinthians 7**

Galatians 3:1–14

Saved through Faith Alone

Father, as we read your Word today, allow your Word to be read into our lives.

Paul begins this section of the letter with a rhetorical question. He knew full well who had 'bewitched' the Galatian converts (v 1) and he holds nothing back in his rebuke of their adherence to this false gospel. Paul's argument hinges on the premise that any worth we may glean from the things we do is offensive to the finished work of Christ crucified. Had Paul been penning these words himself, I can picture sparks flying off the page as he unravels his argument.

In what Stott describes as a 'master-stroke',[1] Paul cites Abraham. With the Judaisers looking to Moses as their teacher, Paul rewinds centuries further for the example of one who received the promise through faith alone. Paul is essentially saying that, in contrast to what they were being told, they were already children of Abraham through faith. This would have been an incendiary statement to the Judaisers. In subsequent days we'll observe Paul adding more fuel to this fire.

Paul advances his argument, referring to curses and blessings. His argument to the Galatian converts, and to us today, is that we must abandon any suggestion that we can make ourselves acceptable to God in any way other than relying on the finished work of Christ. We need to come, once again, on our knees to the cross of Christ and lean on his mercy. In that way, as Paul will uncover, the blessing of Abraham astonishingly becomes ours. Take a moment to ponder on verse 14 and ask the Father to touch you afresh with the Spirit, which is all made possible because of the finished work of the Son.

Give thanks to God that if you've accepted Christ, you are an inheritor of the promises given to Abraham.

[1] John Stott, *Only One Way*, IVP, 1974, p72

BIBLE IN A YEAR: **2 Samuel 17,18; Psalms 52–54**

From Curse to Blessing

'Twas grace that taught my heart to fear,/ and grace my fears relieved'.[1]

Paul continues his argument against ethnic qualifications or any human contribution being sufficient in attaining the acceptance of God. Though writing to Gentile converts, he does so by reference to the Hebrew Scriptures. Abraham and Moses (the mediator, v 19) are the key characters mentioned. The promise was given to Abraham, the law to Moses. You may find it helpful to consider the law as a tutor – one from whom we learn and receive discipline, but don't live under. Luther, commenting on this passage, notes, 'The simile of the schoolmaster is striking. Schoolmasters are indispensable. But show me a pupil who loves his schoolmaster.'[2]

In this section of the letter, Paul builds on the argument that he began earlier (v 7) regarding the Gentile claim to the promises of Abraham. God had promised Abraham that through his seed all the families of the world would be blessed.[3] Paul makes it clear here that the seed, or offspring, of Abraham is not referring to a specific ethnic group of people but rather to a single person, namely Jesus Christ. Consequently, inheritors of the promise are those who are found in Christ. This is wonderful news to the Gentile believers in Galatia – and to us too.

As in a covenantal agreement, such as a will, the promise of God is binding. Each who has trusted in Christ for salvation has received the blessing of eternal life and the promises made to Abraham. The law has highlighted our need of Christ, but (as Paul remarks) it has pronounced us guilty. However, as Paul writes, 'when the kindness and love of God our Saviour appeared, he saved us, not because of righteous things we had done, but because of his mercy.'[4]

Consider what it means to be a recipient of the promises of God. Ask God for the courage to take a firm grip on all that is yours.

---

[1] John Newton, 1779, 'Amazing Grace' [2] Quoted by David Guzik's commentary, enduringword.com/bible-commentary/ [3] Gen 12:7 [4] Titus 3:4,5

BIBLE IN A YEAR: **2 Samuel 19,20; 1 Corinthians 8**

From Bondage to Freedom

Take a moment to thank God that you can approach him as 'Father'.

I wonder if you've noticed a shift in focus as Paul moves from talking in the first person plural ('we') to the privileged position of the Galatian Christians ('you')? '*We* were held in custody under the law' (see v 23) – '*You* are all children of God' (see v 26). In a declaration that would have lit the touchpaper back then and still does today, Paul states, 'If you belong to Christ, then you are Abraham's seed' (v 29). This is the heart of Paul's argument throughout the letter: whether you are a Jewish or Gentile believer in Christ, you are the heir of the promises of God. Consequently, Paul can say that there is neither Jew nor Gentile (v 28): you either belong to Christ or not.

Having covered the Jew versus Gentile debates, Paul then moves on to discussing slavery, specifically as a metaphor for life outside of Christ, life in bondage to the law and the 'elemental spiritual forces of the world' (4:3). Imagine slaves being adopted as children into the family they once served. Paul is saying that Christ came to liberate slaves and change their status to children. This is astonishingly good news for the whole world. As when the disciples of Jesus asked how they should pray,[1] Paul reiterates that when we pray, we can say, '*Abba*, Father' (4:6). Moreover, not only can we address God as 'Father' but, remarkably, we have the status of heirs. I recall a preacher once defining the inheritance that Paul alludes to as 'a secure possession, which is ours now and can never be taken away'. As Christians, we can easily fall into the trap of believing that what we have in Christ will one day be revealed. However, unlike an earthly inheritance that may be yours at some future point, what *you* have in Christ is yours now. May 'Abba' give us the courage to reach out and take hold of it.

What is yours that you're yet to grasp, as a child of God? Hold out your hands and ask God to show you the extent of what is yours.

[1] Luke 11:1,2

BIBLE IN A YEAR: **2 Samuel 21,22; 1 Corinthians 9**

Galatians 4:8–20

Abba, Father...

Father, remind us today of the freedom we can have in you.

A few years ago, on the Pacific coast of North America, animal-rights activists managed to set a whale free from an aquarium beside the ocean. What happened next was remarkable. The whale swam some distance, spent a short time at sea and then returned voluntarily to the aquarium. It had decided that it was better off being looked after in captivity than fending for itself in the dangerous and difficult world outside. Paul here laments that the Galatian Christians had turned back to weak and miserable principles,[1] preferring slavery over freedom (v 9).

The issue highlighted now is the observance of special festivals. What is the problem here? After all, don't we all celebrate and enjoy special days? The Galatians were observing Jewish festivals, the point being that in doing so they looked forward to the great act of redemption that God *would one day accomplish*. The whole point of the gospel that they had accepted was that he *already had accomplished* it.

Since the start of the letter, Paul has articulated a step-by-step theological argument. At verse 12 he is like a lecturer in full teaching mode: he pauses, takes off his glasses and has a heart-to-heart moment with the students. Initially, Paul reminisces on the level of care they'd shown to him in the past. Then comes the piercing question, 'Where, then, is your blessing of me now?' (v 15). How Paul longs for them to savour once more the freedom they'd discovered, rather than the retreat back to a form of captivity. It would do us all well to pause for a moment and assess the joy we've known in our faith journey and how it compares with what we feel now.

I wonder if the joy question made you sit up and take notice, as it did me? Ask Abba to restore something that may have become diluted over time.

---

[1] Gal 4:9 ESV

BIBLE IN A YEAR: **2 Samuel 23,24; 1 Corinthians 10**

Galatians 4:21–31

Sarah and Hagar...

Lord, help me to hear today how loved, accepted and cherished I am.

How do you feel, having read those verses? If you're like me, you may have needed to take a second look to follow the thread of Paul's reasoning. My head aches a little and if you're somewhat perplexed, then you're in good company. Stott refers to these verses as the most difficult in the letter, presupposing a knowledge of the Old Testament which few people possess.[1] Stott, himself, is a notable exception. Paul here uses a familiar story from Genesis that relates to people of slavery and promises. There are three stages to his argument: historical (vs 22,23), allegorical (vs 24–27) and personal (vs 28–31).

You may well be familiar with the stories of Hagar and Sarah. Hagar was the slave woman who bore Ishmael, while Sarah bore Isaac, the child of promise. Allegorically, Paul likens Hagar both to Mount Sinai (where the law was given) and, provocatively, to the present city of Jerusalem. Once again, Paul is presenting an argument that would enrage those seeking to insist on aspects of Judaism as a requisite to being a true Christian. Comparing their holy city of Jerusalem to the mother of Ishmael can be added to the growing list of accusations Paul aims at the Judaisers.

What can we take from these verses? We can rejoice that we are heirs of the Old Testament promises, not subject to slavery but rather children of promise. Contrary to those who had 'bewitched' the Galatians,[2] Paul here emphasises that the true heirs of the promises of Abraham are not defined by physical descent (the Jews). Rather, the true heirs are children of God by spiritual descent, those who have put their faith in Christ, whether Jew or Gentile.

These verses may have been hard to understand. Ask the Lord to give you a level of understanding and don't be discouraged if it doesn't all seem crystal clear.

[1] John Stott, *Only One Way*, IVP, 1974, p121   [2] Gal 3:1

BIBLE IN A YEAR: **1 Kings 1,2; Psalm 55**

Galatians 5:1–12

What is Freedom?

Father, give me the courage to allow you today to take hold of my hand and guide the reins.

Having free rein gives a horse the liberty of unrestricted movement. Is this the type of freedom that Paul is highlighting for the Galatians? In the contemporary Western culture in which I live, people pursue freedom, rarely denying themselves any desire. Everything is permissible as long as it doesn't harm anyone else. This is a false type of freedom and not what Paul is alluding to. Paul longs for the Galatians to experience a freedom from the exhausting pursuit of having to do enough to earn the favour of God.

The legalists who have infiltrated the community are advocating that you can have both Jesus and a law-relationship with God. As Calvin noted, 'Whoever wants to have a half-Christ loses the whole'.[1] At the root of his argument, as we've seen throughout the letter, is Paul's sorrow that the Galatians were leaving Jesus for the teachings of legalism.

Once again, Paul uses the example of circumcision, noting that should a man insist on this then he is beholden to the whole law. Paying your taxes is no defence for a speeding infringement. While Paul's point is clear, we do detect hope in verse 10. All is not lost, and Paul is confident of two things. First, that those to whom he writes will respond positively to his appeal and, second, that those who are sowing confusion will be judged appropriately. Indeed, Paul's indignation reaches an apogee as he expresses a desire for those who are insisting on circumcision to take the knife and use it for emasculation – we won't dwell on this now!

Thank God today that in his mercy he is willing to offer such freedom – but find comfort that his hand is close to the rein should he need to take hold for our protection.

Ponder the times when you've misused the freedom that is yours. Ask God to forgive as necessary and live in the true freedom on offer.

---

[1] Charles Partee, *The Theology of John Calvin*, Presbyterian Publishing Corporation, 2008, p231

BIBLE IN A YEAR: **1 Kings 3–5; 1 Corinthians 11**

Keeping in Step

Father, on this wonderful Pentecost Sunday, give me the courage today to be open to the ministry of your life-giving Spirit.

What a wonderful passage to consider on this particular day!

The second half of this letter is focused on the reality that, in Christ, life is freedom, having secured release from the bondage of the law. However, Paul repeatedly warns how such freedom can be easily lost. In this wonderful section of the letter, he emphasises that the only way to be truly free is by keeping 'in step' with the Holy Spirit (v 25). I was fascinated by watching the procession following Queen Elizabeth II's hearse on the day of her funeral in September 2022. Of the thousands marching, I didn't spot anyone at any point marching out of step.

Paul gives a detailed list of what it looks like to be out of step with God's best. He describes these behaviours as desires of the sinful nature. As you consider the list (vs 19–21) you will see that many of these things seem to come naturally to us. There is a better way, that Paul says is in direct contradiction to our sinful nature. This internal battle that wages within us is more fully described by Paul in his letter to the Romans.[1] Like me, you may read this and feel frustrated that what sounds so wonderful is so much more challenging to live out. Why not take a moment to read some words from one of Paul's other letters? In Philippians, he encourages his readers to fix their minds on certain things – and to put into practice what they have learned.[2] I'm convinced that, as we repeatedly engage in virtues pleasing to the Holy Spirit, these virtues will, in time, become a natural part of us. None of the marchers at the funeral would have got up that morning and joined the procession having never marched before!

Take a moment for introspection. Look at the contrasting list in this passage. Ask God to turn you from destructive behaviour towards the light of his presence.

[1] Rom 7 [2] Phil 4:8,9

BIBLE IN A YEAR: **1 Kings 6,7; 1 Corinthians 12**

Galatians 6:1–10

I Want to Break Free!

Lord, thank you so much for your kindness that leads us to repentance.

I wonder when you last found yourself caught or trapped by something. An initial glance at verse 1 may prompt you to think of someone being caught doing something sinful, akin to the adulterous woman presented to Jesus by the Pharisees.[1] The reference to 'being caught' translates to being surprised at either being discovered in sinning or actually committing the sin. You can probably identify people for whom entrapment has been overwhelming. Some of you will have or may still be experiencing it yourself. Paul makes it clear, as does the wider narrative of Scripture, that escape is possible and that we are called to be involved in the restoration process.

I recall as a child falling deeply into a thorn bush: escaping from the branches that enveloped me was not as simple as going out the way I came in. A slow, painful, but gentle removal of the thorns and branches by those who were with me led eventually to my being free. It took time and the scars remained for quite some while. Paul urges the Galatian believers to bear each other's burdens. As the people of God, we must ensure that we gently remove sharp thorns from those who are caught in something, rather than accentuate the discomfort. Just as Jesus carried the cross for you and wore thorns that pierced his brow, so must we be willing to help carry the load that others may be bearing. How about being proactive in looking for the opportunity that Paul mentions in the final verse of today's reading? Who is there today in your line of sight to whom you could offer some words of hope and encouragement?

Think of someone (it may be you) who is caught or trapped. Pray for them, asking for a gentle release. Could you be a part of the process of restoration?

[1] John 8:1–11

BIBLE IN A YEAR: **1 Kings 8,9; Psalms 56,57**

Galatians 6:11–18

PS What Compels You?

Father, help us today to find our desires corresponding with your will.

Today's reading is the postscript of the letter. There is much speculation around what Paul meant by his reference to 'large letters' (v 11). Rightly or wrongly, I like to think that these 'large letters' are the equivalent of using bold print to emphasise a point. Lightfoot comments, 'He writes in large bold characters, that his handwriting may reflect the energy and determination of his soul.'[1]

In this postscript we find ourselves again immersed in the argument that weaves its way throughout the entire letter. Paul emphasises one final time that our standing before God is dependent on what he has done for us and not on anything impressive that we may have done. In fact, one of the biggest burdens we can carry is the overwhelming desire to impress others. This may sound crude, but the Judaisers sought to wear a badge of honour based on how many Gentile foreskins were cut off! After all, that was a boast of one of their heroes, King David.[2] The word 'compel' (v 12) is critical in our consideration of these verses, and indeed the whole letter. After all, circumcision is not a sin, but Paul's angst is targeted at those who compelled the new Galatian converts of its necessity in being accepted by God. Has much really changed? I urge you not to feel pressurised if someone in the life of your church encourages you to do something on the basis that it will somehow earn God's favour.

Paul ends his letter in the same way as it began. Having argued, rebuked and corrected, his final word is 'grace' (v 18). May you too know the grace of our Lord Jesus Christ, who has made it possible for your sin to be crucified and his righteousness to become yours.[3] What a Saviour!

May the grace of the Lord Jesus Christ be yours and may you know the comfort of his Spirit.

---

[1] JB Lightfoot, *St Paul's Epistle to the Galatians*, Macmillan, 1865, p211,212 [2] Cf 1 Sam 18:27 [3] 2 Cor 5:21

BIBLE IN A YEAR: **1 Kings 10,11; 1 Corinthians 13**

Vivien Whitfield

SOMETHING ABOUT MYSELF – AND THE BIBLE

Vivien Whitfield talks about her faith journey, her time in ministry and the ways the Bible has supported her and impacted her through life.

I spent the first ten months of my life in a small village in Hertfordshire where my grandfather was the rector. I like to think it's possible that George Bernard Shaw saw me in my pram, as he lived there. Being an atheist, he apparently had many arguments with Grandpa!

My family moved to Wallington (in Surrey, now Greater London), where I grew up. When I was nine I joined the Brownies in an evangelical church, which we eventually made our church, and I began to learn a lot from the Bible in the Kings Own group (for children) and then Pathfinders (for teenagers). It was a very missionary-minded church and my first sense of calling to the service of God came during that time. I was given a Jungle Doctor book as a prize while in Kings Own (I still have it!) and was determined to become a nurse and work with him in Africa! (It didn't happen, but was a start, at least!) I became a committed Christian in my teens, during my confirmation classes. We young people were encouraged to attend evensong, and I learned a lot through the very biblically based sermons there.

After A-levels I trained as a primary-school teacher and taught for about 12 years before God touched me again about missionary service and I went to All Nations Christian College. I loved the lectures there – I can remember feeling really excited in a module on Exodus (I think it was) and seeing new things that opened up the Bible to me. From there I went to Peru in 1982 with what was then the Evangelical Union of South America, which later became Latin Link. My main work was training local church leaders, including teaching in the local Night Bible Institute (in Spanish, of course). This was at a very basic level, because most students barely had more than primary-school education, but the aim was to help them develop a Bible-based ministry.

I finally returned to the UK in 1991 because of encroaching deafness (which made it very difficult to minister in a second language!) and moved to Colchester, Essex. I later rejoined Latin Link, encouraging churches to think biblically about mission, until I retired in 2006. Among other things around that time, I also did a couple of theological degrees (my supervisor for my MA dissertation was another *Encounter with God* writer, Mary Evans!).

As my deafness worsened I began to learn some British Sign Language; later I was invited to join the diocesan Deaf Ministry team, reaching out to those who had a very negative view of the Bible since at their special boarding schools they'd been made to sit through church services

they couldn't hear or understand – and anyway the Bible was just for hearing people, wasn't it? (God spoke, God heard, but God never seemed to sign...)

I had joined my local parish church, and to have some clout as a minister among deaf people I was fast-tracked to become a Reader (later commuted to be a Licensed Lay Minister). More recently, after about fourteen years of deaf ministry, I have opted out of the team. This is primarily because during the Covid pandemic, when we couldn't meet face to face, my signing skills deteriorated – and they'd never been good anyway!

In 2012, when I had almost no natural hearing left, I was offered a cochlear implant (thank you, NHS!), which has helped immeasurably with hearing conversations and environmental sounds, but plays havoc with music, severely affecting sung worship for me. So if anything, the Bible has been even more of a lifeline for me!

For several years I also did some distance tutoring for St John's College,

Vivien Whitfield

Nottingham, in both Old Testament and New Testament. I was first invited to write for *Encounter* for notes that came out in 2013. So the Bible was pretty central in all I was doing then.

In 2016, during a chat with my vicar, I was challenged (not for the first time!) to be ordained, and despite my age it felt right this time. Again I was fast-tracked because of my theological training and Christian ministry experience; I was ordained deacon in 2017 and priest in 2018. I was locally deployed and, of course, non-stipendiary, and I did my three-year curacy in my own church. I then became the church's Associate Vicar for a year; but after that the rules said I could no longer be licensed (too old; I was 75 by then). However, I was given PTO (Permission To Officiate) and have continued with much of what I was doing anyway! So much of church ministry is Bible-centred, of course. I particularly enjoy preaching from the Bible when I'm given the opportunity, and many of our church members have appreciated the background I can bring in my sermons, which opens up God's Word to them in new ways. It's lovely to be able to give something back, after all I received from earlier preachers and teachers.

Memories and key moments

Apart from learning Bible stories at primary school, my first hands-on memories of the Bible were through doing 'sword drill' at Kings Own as a child; we were given a reference to look up and the first one to find it held up our Bible in the air and read out the verse to show we had won. That definitely helped me learn to find my way around the Bible!

When I was 12 I started reading the Bible daily, using the notes that my mother used: one of SU's publications – I think it was *Daily Bread*, though I may have that wrong. I've rarely missed a day since, trying different methods to help me, and I currently use *Encounter* myself. So Scripture Union has nearly always been part of my devotional life, along with the encouragement I received from my Pathfinder leaders who taught me a lot as a teenager and brought me to the point of committing my life to Jesus. I'm still in touch with one of them!

'[I] knew God to be my rock and refuge and that I could trust him and pour out my heart to him.'

There have been a few key moments when the Word was especially significant to me. To name just four: Psalm 40:1–3 was highly significant when the Lord brought me back to himself after a black patch; he took me out of the bog I was in and set my feet on a rock, putting a new song in my mouth. It says it all! I obeyed his call to be a missionary after that! Then 2 Thessalonians 1:11,12 also spoke to me very clearly about my missionary call, while I was sitting on the floor in a corridor at a conference centre around midnight. Much later, when I was diagnosed with early breast cancer, I turned to Psalm 62 and knew God to be my rock and refuge and that I could trust him and pour out my heart to him. That's still stuck to the side of my wardrobe in my 'God corner'! More recently still, during my exploration regarding ordination, it was 2 Corinthians 9:8 that was my special verse. I sensed that God was promising to provide all I needed to do the work to which he was calling me.

And now?
I think what excites me most about the Bible is how incredibly relevant it is. Notes I wrote for *Encounter* on 1 Samuel during the worst of the COVID pandemic seemed to speak so clearly to the world's pain. I'm currently writing on 1 Chronicles and seeing how the chronicler's sermon is just as relevant to twenty-first-century Christians as to his readers of the fourth century BC. And I've always loved the prophets' emphasis on justice and committed faith – again, so incredibly relevant to our own times.

If you'd like to pray for me, please pray that I will be faithful to the end, whenever that may be. By the time this is printed I shall be in my late seventies, and I'm already feeling some of the effects of ageing. I would like to be able to continue a Bible ministry for a few more years yet!

A SERMON FOR OUR TIME

These readings present a challenge for today's reader. Not only do they include some nasty stuff, but we might rightly claim that our world is different from theirs. However, as Wilcock points out, that's exactly what makes us today the kind of audience the chronicler meant to address.[1] The two books of Chronicles were originally one volume, which was probably written in the fourth century BC. We don't know who wrote it. Its first readers were subjects of the Persian Empire, descendants of those who had been restored to their homeland in Judah after the Exile of the sixth century BC. For them, nearly everything in the book was part of an age gone by, so they could well have found it a dead book. They might have found it dry bones to read, but in their own context they needed a fresh breath of life and the chronicler knew that a message from the past could bring that. It could, of course, simply be seen as an alternative reading, a retelling of the stories of Samuel and Kings, but with a lot left out and quite a bit added by a writer who seems to have had some bees in his bonnet and a tendency to exaggerate.[2] However, it's a lot more than that. It's a sermon – and very relevant to our own time.

All good sermons have an aim in mind: the aim here was to foster a right relationship between God and his people, to show how failure and judgement could lead to grace and restoration. God's inflexible justice is always present, but so are his divine grace, his mercy and his steadfast love. As we read the book, particularly as we think about David's life and reign, we will see examples of this and how those for whom David is long gone can learn some important truths. Principles derived from the past presented a mirror to the first readers and they do to us too. So stay with it, and let God teach you!

Vivien Whitfield

---

[1] Michael Wilcock, *The Message of Chronicles*, IVP, 1987, p16 [2] Wilcock, 1987, p14

1 Chronicles 10

The Death of a King

As I begin these readings, open my heart, Lord, to hear your voice and respond.

Welcome to a challenging set of readings! The context is the Exile and the subsequent restoration, of the chronicler's own time. His readers would quite likely have found it a dead book, just as we might on initial reading. So many names – and they had all died long before – several hundred years before.[1] It depicted an age gone by. We may ask what relevance it had for them. And for us? But they needed the message – and so do we!

The chronicler was a preacher, not a historian. He aimed to foster a right relationship between God and his people. His writing was therefore selective; he minimised the baddies and emphasised the goodies. After nine chapters of names and genealogies which hint at Israel's history so far, he devotes only one chapter to the renegade Saul and quickly passes to David. Despite many achievements during his reign, Saul had failed, in the chronicler's eyes, and had come under judgement. He was disobedient and had shown disloyalty to God. He therefore faced catastrophe. He died because of his unfaithfulness (v 13).

Sadly, Saul's sin affected others too, including his son Jonathan who died in the battle along with his father and many others. Jonathan was a good guy and a sore loss to David.[2] 'No man is an island, entire of itself', wrote John Donne. Our actions and attitudes can affect others more than we might think. Is this perhaps a wake-up call for us? Is there anything that you're currently involved in which is perhaps riding roughshod over other people? Perhaps a decision affecting the family? Perhaps the way you travel or shop? Allow the Lord to put a searchlight on you.

Lord, it's so easy to act first and think afterwards. Help me to be aware of the effect of my activities on others and be willing to change.

---

[1] Michael Wilcock, *The Message of Chronicles*, IVP, 1987, p13 [2] See David's lamentation in 2 Sam 1:17–27

BIBLE IN A YEAR: **1 Kings 12,13; 1 Corinthians 14**

Much-Needed Support!

Lord, help me to recognise if I need to be more loyal and supportive to my church leaders.

Any leader needs a good team around them. Yes, David was anointed king over Israel – all that time ago – but he couldn't function without some loyal and brave supporters. We read their names: Joab, Jashobeam, Eleazar, Abishai, Benaiah and the rest (and a lot more in verses 26–47), but how much did the original readers know about them – they had been dead for so long? Even David was only a lost dream; by their time, there wasn't a king like him in existence. Obviously some stories were handed down: the story of a lion in a snowy pit (v 22) would have stuck in the corporate memory. On the whole, however, they possibly knew no more than we do. So why did the chronicler include these names?

Even without a king, Israel still had leaders who needed support in the chronicler's time, whether they were at the top or not. We too are encouraged to remember that the part we play in God's service is valued, even if we're not at the top in terms of up-front ministry. David had 'the three' (v 12) and 'the thirty' (v 15) behind him, but there were long lists of others. Jesus had the twelve, out of whom he chose the three,[1] but he also had the women who provided for his and their daily needs. Church leaders have their church councils or equivalent – but every church member who serves in any way is valued, because the leader cannot lead effectively without support.

If you are a church leader, do you let people know they're valued, even if all they do is wash up? Or do you take them for granted? If you are not at the top and your service is behind the scenes, do you realise how important your support is for God's church to function effectively?

Let your church leader know how much you appreciate them. And perhaps offer to serve in some new way?

[1] Peter, James and John

BIBLE IN A YEAR: **1 Kings 14,15; 1 Corinthians 15**

1 Chronicles 12:1–22,38–40

Changing Sides

Which political party do you support? Pray that you may always vote responsibly.

I write at a time when 'Partygate' is in the news – the UK's national leaders accused of breaking their own rules during the coronavirus pandemic and being fined by the police. Unsurprisingly, subsequent local elections clearly demonstrated that many people were no longer loyal to their previous favourite party and switched sides. This was similarly the case at the time when David was chosen as king in place of Saul. People came to him even from Saul's wider family, even when Saul was still in charge (vs 1–22). There must have been some serious questioning going on: 'Which is the man to follow: Saul or David?' It might have been very risky to side with David! However, Saul's leadership was no longer viable. After his death the choice was clear.

What an impressive array of supporters David had! Ambidextrous archers and stone-slingers (v 2), skilled warriors and fast runners (v 8) and maybe even strong swimmers (v 15)! They just kept coming – what an encouragement!

Among all of these, Amasai stands out. The verb used by the chronicler means 'the Spirit of God *clothed himself* with Amasai'.[2] The prophetic message this chief gave (v 18) must have been a huge encouragement to David, as would have been the unity shown as all came together to enthrone him (v 38).

What should we do if someone we have followed proves to be a grave disappointment? Perhaps even a church leader – there are some tragic stories in our own time; stories of abuse or adultery by those who should know better. At what point should our loyalty and supportiveness change sides? Pray for your church leaders! They, perhaps more than most, are under the attack of the devil and vulnerable to temptation.

Lord, help me to think with great clarity when serious issues arise in church or in national life – and to act accordingly.

---

[1] Michael Wilcock, *The Message of Chronicles*, IVP, 1987, p61 [2] Wilcock, 1987, p62

BIBLE IN A YEAR: **1 Kings 16,17; Psalms 58,59**

A Sudden Halt

Pray that God will help you to understand what holiness means.

I lived in Peru for a number of years, and one memory concerns the time when I needed to fit a longer electric cable to an appliance. I needed to measure the length of cable carefully, so to anchor one end I plugged it into a live socket. I then measured up – and cut the cable – bang!! I have had a great respect for electricity ever since!

This story of the carrying of the ark of God from Abinadab's house in Kiriath Jearim to the city of David (Jerusalem) begins with great excitement, joy and genuine worship, but it suddenly ends with a destructive bang, because Uzzah had not understood the danger of overfamiliarity with God. The ark was at the heart of Israelite religion and worship, containing artefacts that dated back to God's meeting with his people at Sinai.[1] It had a lot of spiritual meaning, and Uzzah's attitude to it should have been as reverent as his attitude to God himself. Perhaps he'd grown used to its presence during the 20 years it had been at his father's house[2] and he failed to understand that destruction or blessing was linked to a realisation of what it was and a respect for holy things.

It's not surprising that David's anger turned to fear (v 12). Are there things in our own Christian culture which we have perhaps failed to treat as holy? Some Quechua Christians in Peru will not put a Bible on the floor. It's not a case of superstition, but of respect. In our emphasis on God's love, are we guilty of being overfamiliar with him, forgetting that he is also holy? How can we distinguish between genuine respect for holy things (Bibles? Communion vessels?) and superstition?

Pray that God will reveal to you any lack of respect that needs your repentance.

---

[1] See Heb 9:1–5 [2] 1 Sam 7:1,2; 2 Sam 6:3

BIBLE IN A YEAR: **1 Kings 18,19; 1 Corinthians 16**

Psalm 137

Outpouring of Anger

What makes you really angry? Talk to God about it.

I often find it hard to watch the news. As the streams of refugees grow longer daily, escaping from unrelenting and unimaginable horrors, this psalm begins to make sense. Those remembering Zion (Jerusalem) have returned from Exile but cannot forget the terror they lived through as they witnessed horrific atrocities before their city was finally razed and burnt by the Babylonians. They were then forcibly removed to a strange land, gloated over by the Edomites (v 7)[1] and, if that was not bad enough, their worship was mocked.

Their reaction? We might wish that verses 7–9 were not in our Bibles, and of course the New Testament has a lot to say about forgiveness. However, it is right to express anger when something is wrong and hateful to God. CS Lewis recounts, in the Second World War, a train compartment full of young soldiers disbelieving what they'd read about the cruelties of the Nazi regime, assuming it was government propaganda. Lewis says that not to see the wickedness of publishing propaganda 'argues a terrifying insensibility'.[2] The absence of anger and indignation is alarming. God has an implacable hostility – not to the sinner, but to the sin. Kidner suggests we need to receive the impact of this psalm and that 'to cut this witness out of the Old Testament would be to impair its value as revelation, both of what is in man and of what the cross was required to achieve for our salvation'.[3]

We can be sure that there will finally be divine retribution. The phrase 'happy are...' (vs 8,9, TNIV) anticipates Revelation 18:20, when the entire anti-God system symbolised by Babylon finally falls. Note, however, that it is God who ensures justice. Our part is to lay our anger and grief at his feet.

Pray for those living in harrowing conditions.

[1] See Obad 10–14 [2] CS Lewis, *Reflections on the Psalms*, Fount, 1977, p25
[3] Derek Kidner, *Psalms 73–150*, TOTC, IVP, 1975, p461

BIBLE IN A YEAR: **1 Kings 20,21; Nahum 1–3**

Worldly Success

What do you feel is your greatest weakness? Talk to God about it.

The chronicler lays it on thick! David is showered with gifts from King Hiram (v 1); his kingdom is 'highly exalted' (v 2); he demonstrates power by expanding the number of his wives and children (v 3 – dubious in our estimation, but that was then!); and he easily overcomes the enemy, the Philistines, as God leads him – in great detail (vs 8–16). What a king! It all sounds too good to be true! Indeed, in David's time Israel's territory stretched for some three hundred miles, with a great king, the best of armies and an immense reputation. By the chronicler's time that was all gone, pared down to almost nothing. So why did he keep on about the greatness of the past in his sermon? Wilcock reminds us that some of the most outstanding Old Testament characters, such as Daniel, living in exile with no land of their own, fearlessly declared that the Most High (not Babylon or Persia) was sovereign over all. Wilcock stresses that the power of God, which made David so successful, was revealed in another way in the Exile, when David's descendants no longer had any power of their own.[1]

Paul also discovered that the Lord's power is made perfect in weakness.[2] This is so encouraging for us, who often feel weak when faced with an unbelieving world that scorns our faith one minute and is indifferent the next. As the chronicler's readers discovered, we do not need to be successful, just faithful.

Bearing all this in mind, how do these verses speak to you? How important are earthly trappings for you and for your sense of self-worth? If things are going well for you, how do you see God's power at work? If you are struggling and feel stripped of earthly wealth and success, how do you see God's power at work?

Talk to God honestly about your answers to those questions.

---

[1] Eg Dan 5:17–21; Michael Wilcock, *The Message of Chronicles*, IVP, 1987, p81 [2] 2 Cor 12:9

BIBLE IN A YEAR: **1 Kings 22; Psalms 60,61**

1 Chronicles 15:1 – 16:6

Exuberant Worship

'O worship the Lord in the beauty of holiness! / Bow down before him, his glory proclaim!'[1]

Can you remember a time when you were 'lost in wonder, love and praise' as the old hymn puts it?[2] Perhaps your worship is usually more restrained than that. Certainly David knew what abundant joy could be experienced through exuberant worship. Worship is a lot more than simply emotion, but emotion plays a part. It is a lot more than simply meaningful words and music, but they play a part. I write as someone no longer able to appreciate music since becoming deafened, but I can find the joy of worship in other ways.

David got it right this time, and all went well with the transfer of the ark to Jerusalem. Why, though, did the chronicler focus so much on the ark when in his own time – post-Exile – it wasn't there? It had disappeared in the chaos when Jerusalem was sacked. Israel had since rebuilt the Temple, restored the priesthood and recommenced sacrifices, but they didn't have the central focus that David had. However, says the chronicler in his sermon, what matters is not the ark itself but the truth it enshrined. Five times in our passage it is called 'the ark of the covenant' (15:25,26,28,29; 16:6), reminding his readers of the foundational agreement made in Moses' time at Mount Sinai, when God promised that he would be their God and they his people. His name, Yahweh (the LORD, printed in small capitals in English translations; eg 15:2,3,12,13,14,15), was his covenant name.

For us, the key to all meaningful worship is the new covenant relationship we have with God through the blood of Jesus.[3] However lustily (and loudly!) we may sing and play, however energetically we may dance before the Lord, however piously we may perform our ritual worship, it counts for nothing without such a relationship with God.

What stimulates you to worship God from the heart? How can you develop your capacity for worship?

---

[1] John SB Monsell, 1811–75 [2] Charles Wesley, 1707–88, 'Love divine, all loves excelling' [3] Matt 26:28

BIBLE IN A YEAR: **2 Kings 1–3; Habakkuk 1–3**

Arranging Worship

'O give thanks to the LORD'.[1] Do that, as you prepare to read his Word.

Asaph has been appointed as worship director (vs 4,5,7) and he begins by using the psalms. A good move! There's a psalm for every occasion and every mood – laments and praise and much more. Sadly, it seems that fewer churches make use of the psalms in their worship these days. Have we lost something precious? This song of praise ranges from Psalm 105:1–15 (a celebration of God's works and words, vs 8–22), through Psalm 96 (which praises his greatness and worth, vs 23–33) to Psalm 106:1,47,48 (a personal cry in which the singers apply the covenant to themselves, vs 34–36).

The emphasis is very much on *God's* works and words, including his promise of land as an inheritance (vs 15–18) and his protection of his people when they were vulnerable (vs 19–22). It was indeed a covenant of grace – God would do these things for them, simply because he loved them and not because they deserved anything.[2] When we worship, do the words we use reflect the fact that we are utterly dependent on our bountiful, generous God and that we are forgiven sinners who deserve nothing? Or are some of our worship songs rather too me-centred?

The final verses of the chapter detail the responsibilities David assigned to suitably gifted people, to enable worship to happen as it should, whether in Jerusalem or at Gibeon. In our own day, of course, such details will be very different. Have you ever given thought to how much work goes on behind the scenes to enable you to worship each Sunday and how many different people (mostly volunteers!) are involved? One might imagine a church leader today saying, 'and Ruth will be worship director; Martin can be in charge of the PA system; the band can be led by Wendy...'

Who are those in your own church who hold such positions of responsibility? Do you pray for them?

---

[1] Ps 136:1, RSV [2] Cf Deut 7:7,8

BIBLE IN A YEAR: **2 Kings 4,5; Zephaniah 1–3**

The Significance of Place

Come into God's presence, trusting him for your future.

There's a particular place in the foothills of the Andes in southern Peru which will always be significant for me. It's where I talked with God and made the decision to return to the UK after several years of mission work in the country, because of encroaching deafness. Places can be important to people for all sorts of reasons, marking significant moments in their lives. David had the laudable desire to provide a permanent place for the ark of God, which, as we've already noted, was highly meaningful for God's people then.

Of course God doesn't need a static house, although buildings such as churches and cathedrals can often provide those significant moments of encounter with God. God allowed David to have the idea, but it would be his son Solomon who eventually built the Temple (vs 11–14).[1] Right now, however, God had bigger 'house' plans for David (vs 10b,11) and promised to do the building work himself. The house of David would culminate in David's descendant Jesus – and where Jesus is, is still the most significant place to be!

Have you ever had a strong desire to do something special for God, only to find that God himself disallows it? Perhaps he uses circumstances, and you realise it's an impossible task. Maybe that's because God has bigger plans for you; plans to use you in ways you cannot imagine at the moment. When I was earnestly praying through whether I should leave Peru, a good friend suggested that God would have something even better for me to do back home. She was right! Although at the time I felt thrown on the rubbish heap, no longer fit to do anything for God because I was going deaf, I discovered over time that even profound deafness is no barrier to God's using me.

Does this speak to you? Be encouraged! God has something even better in view for you!

[1] 1 Kings 6

BIBLE IN A YEAR: **2 Kings 6,7; Haggai 1,2**

An Honour Indeed!

As you come to read God's Word, focus on how he knows you inside out!

Have you, or someone you know, been honoured by your monarch, or head of state or equivalent, with a medal for services rendered? In most cases such news comes as a big surprise, even met with incredulity. Nathan had delivered God's message to David. God was honouring him! Now David responded. We sense astonishment, amazement. John Newton echoed this feeling as he penned the hymn 'Amazing grace'[1] many years after coming to realise what God had done for him, eventually bringing him out of slave-trading and into Christian ministry. We often sing those words, but do we truly sense the amazement that God has 'saved a wretch like me'? Do we echo David's astonishment? Or has the story become so familiar that we barely give it a thought? Furthermore, David was aware that God knew what he was truly like (v 18), which made the astonishment even greater. And 'yes, please!' was his answer (v 23).

This passage, however, is not just about the king. David brings in the whole of God's people and what had been done for them too (vs 21,22). In a similar way, God's saving work in us as individuals is inextricably linked with what he is doing in and through his church, all over the world. That's huge! Do you have any inkling about how God might be using you to further his purposes? When you think about it, that is a tremendous honour!

Interspersed with David's words of amazement are hints of worship: 'There is no one like you' (v 20); 'your name will be great for ever' (v 24). When we think how well God knows us and when we realise just how much he has done for us – despite who we are – does this lead only to astonishment, or also to worship?

If you know Newton's hymn, sing it with renewed consciousness and thanksgiving.

---

[1] John Newton, 1725–1807, 'Amazing grace! How sweet the sound / that saved a wretch like me'

BIBLE IN A YEAR: **2 Kings 8,9; Psalms 62,63**

1 Chronicles 18

Enemy? Or Supporter?

Pray into today's news. How does the world look from God's perspective?

Much of this makes us feel very uncomfortable. David was continuing what had been commanded earlier because of the Canaanites' religious iniquity,[1] so that such evil would not spread, preventing Israel from being God's light in the world. McConville says, 'The slaughter of the Canaanites cannot but be repugnant to the modern reader. But perhaps … it can be seen as the dark, other side of God's love, a love that is solemn, even fierce, but whose end is the salvation of the world.'[2] It does not give us a mandate for that kind of treatment today!

The chronicler omits the family strife, immorality and murder which marred David's reign and which we read about in 2 Samuel. Here, he is focusing on David the king, rather than the man.[3] It's all about the reputation and influence of his glorious kingdom. For the chronicler's readers, however, all that glory had gone. Their existence was dominated by pagan empires. Church history tells us of attempts to make the church the glorious kingdom of Christ, but we know all too well that from a secular point of view it means nothing for many today.

It is noteworthy that even amid David's enemies – the nations hostile to him – there were some individuals who came into his service: Tou, king of Hamath (vs 9,10) and some of the Kerethites and Pelethites (from Goliath's home town).[4] Today, many oppose the King of kings, but many accept him and his fame is still going out into all lands. When you read the news of horrific things happening in the world and you wonder where God is, be encouraged. Jesus *is* building his kingdom and those of us who have voluntarily come into his service have a part to play in this. The world may look a mess, but God's perspective is different.

What part has God called you to play? Does it help you to see things from his perspective?

---

[1] Eg Gen 15:16; Deut 20:16–18 [2] Gordon McConville, *Grace in the End*, Paternoster, 1993, p144
[3] Wilcock, 1987, p78 [4] 2 Sam 15:18; 1 Sam 17:4

BIBLE IN A YEAR: **2 Kings 10–12; Zechariah 1,2**

Relational Prayer

Forgive me, Lord, when my prayers are more automatic than inspired by my relationship with you.

This is the first of a run of eight consecutive psalms attributed to David – either as part of his collection, or as penned by him. It's the kind of psalm he would come up with following the victories outlined in yesterday's reading. The overriding sense is thanksgiving (vs 1–3) – something we often forget when God answers our prayers! My most frequent prayer tends to be 'Lord, help me!' and I try to remember to thank him when he does!

There is expectation here, too (vs 4–6), the realisation that the 'kings of the earth' will also praise the Lord. It reminds us that one day every tongue must confess that Jesus Christ is Lord,[1] as they recognise his wisdom and his glorious sovereignty – and also his care for those humble enough to turn to him (all of which are anticipated in vs 4–6).

Then there is a personal confidence (vs 7,8) that God will deliver and rescue. Of course we know that, humanly speaking, deliverance from trouble doesn't always work out as we would like. Troubles will come, but *in the midst of them* we can be confident of the Lord's right hand to hold us. Then there's the knowledge that, whatever happens, he will fulfil his purposes (v 8). Different English translations of the Bible offer different slants on this: 'The LORD will perfect that which concerneth me' (AV); 'The LORD will vindicate me' (NIV); 'The LORD will fulfil his purpose for me' (NRSV). Each is a very personal statement of faith, based on the psalmist's relationship with God and the knowledge that his steadfast love never dates! After such a wonderful psalm of thanksgiving, expectation and confidence, the final squeak ('do not abandon the works of your hands') reminds us that the psalmist, like us, was very human!

How does the psalm speak to you? Talk to God about it.

[1] Phil 2:9–11

BIBLE IN A YEAR: **2 Kings 13,14; Zechariah 3,4**

1 Chronicles 19:1 – 20:8

Controlling the Nations

'... the earth shall be filled with the glory of God / as the waters cover the sea'.[1] Where do you see that happening?

These two chapters continue the theme the chronicler sought to outline in chapters 14 and 18: that of the fame and fear of the king. Nahash (19:2) had been an enemy of Saul's[2] and thus an ally of David's, but Nahash's son Hanun's advisers deliberately made false accusations. If they had had social media back then they would have had a heyday spreading disinformation! Thanks to Joab, those who had been shamefully and embarrassingly treated were vindicated, but it makes a very unpleasant story.

Comparing chapter 20 with 2 Samuel 11, we discover the consequence of King David staying at home this time instead of going out to battle. Beautiful women have often been the downfall of great leaders. It is vital to pray for our church leaders, who are just as prone to temptation as anyone else. The chronicler ignores this aspect of David's story, although maybe he gives a nod to it by mentioning the unusual fact that David stayed at home. Instead, he focuses on the positives of military success, booty and more workers, which he sees as being illustrative of the glory of David's kingdom. David's enemies were subjugated – even though we know (and the chronicler's readers knew) that his worst enemy was himself!

Just as in chapters 14 and 18, the time *of* which the chronicler writes is a day of great things, but the time *in* which he writes is significantly less so and reminds us that even under foreign dominance God's hand was unmistakably at work behind the scenes. Needless to say, it still is! There is huge uncertainty and fear in our world today, let alone actual suffering, and we must cling on to the truth that the God who helped David is still able to control the nations today, even when it's hard to see it!

What do you fear most when you listen to the news? Bring it to God in honest prayer.

---

[1] AC Ainger, 1841–1919, 'God is working his purpose out' [2] 1 Sam 11

BIBLE IN A YEAR: **2 Kings 15,16; Psalms 64,65**

Incitement to Sin

'... lead us not into temptation, but deliver us from the evil one.'[1]

Have you ever been in the position where you are told by someone in authority to do something which you believe to be wrong? How have you responded? Taking a census of military-age men in Israel was wrong, whether David was incited by Satan (v 1) or – in his anger against Israel – by God.[2] Joab knew this; perhaps he remembered the law of Moses which stipulated that a census would require a half-shekel payment per person as a ransom for their lives, to avoid plague.[3]

Why did David do it? Was he proud of the size of his army? Why did he take so long to realise it was a wrong thing to do? Was he too taken up with Bathsheba?[4] In the harrowing sequence of sin, punishment, realisation and repentance, God overrules the evil and brings about something which could not then be foreseen. The site of Araunah's threshing floor was on

a hill in the area called Moriah,[5] where Abraham had been told to sacrifice Isaac – who was redeemed by a ram[6] – and where later the Lamb of God, the ultimate sacrifice, would die on a cross and finally halt the plague of sin.[7]

Psalm 51 is normally associated with David's penitence over the Bathsheba-Uriah affair, but he must have felt pretty bad to have been responsible for these seventy thousand deaths (v 14). He could only cast himself on God's mercy (vs 13–15). God is still able to overrule evil and bring something good out of it. Wilcock says, 'When we do sin, God can take that sin and its evil effects and transmute them into something that will contribute to his glory.'[8] He reminds us, at the same time, of Paul's warning against deliberately sinning to win God's grace![9]

Is there any sin in your own life which needs to be transformed by God into something good? Confess it and ask for his mercy.

---

[1] Matt 6:13 [2] 2 Sam 24:1 [3] Exod 30:11-16 [4] See 2 Sam 11 [5] 2 Chr 3:1 [6] Gen 22:1-19
[7] Wilcock, 1987, p94–96 [8] Wilcock, 1987, p91 [9] Rom 6:1,2

BIBLE IN A YEAR: **2 Kings 17,18; Zechariah 5,6**

1 Chronicles 22:2–19

Motives Matter

Why do you follow Jesus? Just because of what he has done for you?

I'm not sure what to make of David here. He's not allowed to build the Temple himself (and now we know why, v 8), but he does as much as he can under the pretext of Solomon's youth and inexperience! Many young people would sympathise with Solomon and feel indignant, sensing that David should take his hands off and allow Solomon to do it his way. It's true, however, that David's acceptance of a vast quantity of materials and labour potential – mainly from his heathen neighbours and immigrants – would have helped make Solomon's Temple truly magnificent.[1] Significantly, Solomon spent seven years building the Temple for God and thirteen years building his own house,[2] which says something about him. Sadly, we know that Solomon's initial obedience to David's charge to follow and obey the Lord (vs 12,13) was short-lived. How much was due to having been lavishly provided for, with no threats to peace during his lifetime? How easy it is to ignore God when all is going well!

So how do we react to this chapter? Perhaps the point is that David's chief desire was to make known God's glory and magnificence. Whether or not he was wise to take the steps he did, his overriding motive was for God's glory. However unwise we ourselves might sometimes be – whether in relating to our children or in some other way – it's our motive that finally counts.

What about all those conscripted to contribute? The aliens who were stonecutters, masons, carpenters and artisans (v 15)? Would they have taken pride in their work, knowing that it was for Israel's God? We don't know. It's worth considering, however, that God can use all sorts of people – not just Christians – to do his work.

Where do you see God working in your context through the efforts of non-Christians?

[1] 1 Kings 6 [2] 1 Kings 6:38; 7:1

BIBLE IN A YEAR: **2 Kings 19,20; Zechariah 7,8**

1 Chronicles 23:1–6,24–32

A Future for the Levites?

Consider before God the gifts you bring to his service.

Chapters 23–29 concern the transition from David's years of war and turmoil to a settled existence under Solomon. The Levites were key to the development of a structure that would enable God's people to function well. Up until this point, their main job was to carry the tabernacle and its associated artefacts to enable worship. With the plans to build a Temple, however, those responsibilities would be redundant. David puts in place a new structure. In these next few chapters we read of four categories of Levites who would assist the priests: the staff of the sanctuary (23:7–32), the musicians (ch 25), the gatekeepers (26:1–19) and the officials and judges (26:20–32). This reorganisation of the tribe of Levi was to enable Israel's life to flourish, both spiritually and in other ways.[1]

For the chronicler, of course, this had relevance to his own readers and would have reminded them that in their context they were still to be a people prepared for God's service. By using David's structure for the Levites, as seen through the eyes of the chronicler, Wilcock identifies certain principles for any people emerging from a time of turmoil and being built anew: care, thoroughness, devotion to duty and a sense of community.[2]

As I write, the world is in a mess: the effects of covid and other viruses; climate change producing heat, drought, floods and wild fires; war and unprecedented numbers of refugees… Whether or not we ever emerge into a more settled existence, God's people must still be ready for service. We must still show care and thoroughness as we use our gifts in his service; we must still be wholehearted in devotion to duty; and, very importantly, we need a sense of community. We cannot serve effectively on our own. We need each other.

How has your role in church life changed in recent years? How do you see yourself contributing to God's service now?

[1] For more details, see Wilcock, 1987, p96–107 [2] Wilcock, 1987, p100

BIBLE IN A YEAR: **2 Kings 21,22; Zechariah 9,10**

1 Chronicles 28

Building Plans!

Lord, make me a person you can use for your glory in the church and the world.

Having made plans and organised who does what in the kingdom, David summons everyone with any kind of portfolio to Jerusalem for the official handover to Solomon as king and Temple-builder. David himself is about to die and he now gives to his son the plans he has drawn up – in exquisite detail. (Today's antique dealers would love it!) Importantly, David claims that his plans were given to him by God (v 19).

For the chronicler's readers, it was a reminder that even without David there were important things to learn. They could not complain that the Davidic stories had no relevance for them on the grounds that they lived in a world without him. At this important handover ceremony, David's first concern was to urge everyone to observe and search out – follow – God's ways (v 8); that was something that would never change, even long after David himself had gone. Perhaps, too, in the detail of the plans for the Temple they needed to learn that their own plans must always be aligned with God's plans.

God's detailed plans for the Temple point us to his blueprint for the church. Built upon the foundation of Christ, the 'living Stone', Christians (also 'living stones') are being formed into 'a spiritual house'.[1] Although we can claim the Holy Spirit's help in so forming us, we also have some responsibility as to how we live our lives. Paul talks about building on the foundation (Christ) with gold, silver and precious stones – or merely with wood, hay and straw.[2] Solomon's Temple was ultimately destroyed by the Babylonians, as the chronicler's readers knew well; we today are reminded that the day of judgement will determine the quality of the building materials we are using throughout our lives.

How would you assess the quality of the building materials you are using, as you build on the foundation of Christ? Is there anything that needs to change?

[1] 1 Pet 2:4,5 [2] 1 Cor 3:10–15

BIBLE IN A YEAR: **2 Kings 23–25; Psalms 66,67**

Generous Giving

Thank you, Lord, so much, for all you have given me!

Modern readers might baulk at the way David seems to be showing off here: 'Look at all I've amassed for the Temple – oh, and I'm giving this (huge amount!) from my own purse.' However, leaders need to lead by example, even if less ostentatiously. David was setting an example – and inspiring the assembly to give generously themselves. And along with the generous giving was great joy.

In verse 7 there is a mention of 'darics' of gold. The chronicler's readers may have been bemused by the thought of the lavishness, which was all gone for them, but they would have known the daric: a coin of the Persian Empire, first minted in the reign of Darius I, five centuries after David.[1] The message was very apt for them; they had seen the building (in fits and starts) of the second Temple with the background of later Old Testament prophets urging them to give and get on

with it![2] Israel, after the Exile, faced the same challenge as those of David's time.

Generosity is a measure of thankfulness for God's own generosity. David's prayer in verses 10–19 is heartfelt. Words in verses 11 and 14 have often been used as an offertory prayer in today's churches. Today's temple is made up of people, living stones, as we saw yesterday, but the need is the same: the giving of oneself, expressed by the giving of one's wealth.[3] So the chronicler is preaching to us too. We may not have the vast wealth that David had, but all that we have comes from the Lord and it is of his own that we give him. We can give him nothing that he doesn't first give us – something worth remembering when we're hesitant to be as generous as we might be! And then there's the joy...

Review your giving – and your attitude to it!

[1] Wilcock, 1987, p113 [2] Eg Hag 1:3,4; Mal 3:8–10 [3] 2 Cor 8,9; Acts 11:27–30

BIBLE IN A YEAR: **1 Chronicles 1–3; Zechariah 11,12**

The 'Already' God

Thank you, Lord, that I can be real with you.

What an intensely personal psalm this is! There's no getting away from the God who knows us inside out, better than we can ever know ourselves. Some find this frightening. Others, including myself, find it liberating. I don't have to pretend. Michael Wilcock calls God the 'Already' God. He already knows what we're about to say (v 4); he is already wherever we might wish to go (vs 8–10); I cannot even be who I am without his having already made me 'me' (v 13).[1]

Thinking of the embryo in the womb (v 13), Wilcock adds, 'God ... on that tiny scale was engaged in a task perhaps more like his original immense work of creation than anything else that he does.'[2] No wonder the psalmist cries out that God's thoughts to him are vast and weighty (v 17)! I find it truly wonderful that God is the author of every detail of my being, from conception to death, to the very end of time and onwards into eternity.

Verses 19–22 feel like a sudden switch to us – a black cloud covering the sun, which we would wish wasn't there. It's not like that to the psalmist, however. It sounds disturbing, but it actually reflects the psalmist's zeal for God. He is taking sides against those who are utterly opposed to God and his purposes. He is identifying with God's cause. As we saw in Psalm 137, expressing vehement anger about evil is right, as long as we leave the outcome to God rather than take things into our own hands. In case we might be tempted to do that, the psalmist humbly recognises his own propensity to sin and asks for guidance into the 'way everlasting' (vs 23,24).

Google the James Webb telescope and look at some of the images. Worship the Creator God who knows and loves you so intimately.

---

[1] Michael Wilcock, *The Message of Psalms 73–150*, IVP, 2001, p259 [2] Wilcock, 2001, p260

BIBLE IN A YEAR: **1 Chronicles 4–6; Zechariah 13,14**

King of Kings!

Take your power, O Lord, and reign!

What an epilogue! What joy is expressed here! The sacrifices, the eating and drinking in God's presence, the hope of a glorious future. Everyone lived happily ever after? No! In the account of David's last days in 1 Kings 1 and 2, we see an old man who couldn't get warm, a revolt by his son Adonijah who wanted the throne, a rather hasty coronation of Solomon, some sinister advice concerning Joab – and later we read of Solomon's failures to follow the Lord faithfully. Once again, the chronicler is painting a much happier version by simply omitting the nasty stuff. Why?

He wanted his readers to remember David as he was at the assembly, without clouding the issue. All along, the chronicler had been concerned to focus on the fact that Israel's king ruled under God. Here, Solomon was anointed 'before the LORD' and 'sat on the throne of the LORD' (vs 22,23). Remember what David has just prayed in verse 11: 'Yours, LORD, is the kingdom'. It is God's throne. He is the High King over all. That truth hadn't changed several centuries later. Even in the chronicler's time, when God's people seemed of small account, their God still reigned.[1]

Do we sometimes forget that, when we look at the news? Perhaps this truth – that God still reigns supreme in his world – is the most important thing we can take away with us from these readings. Whatever is happening, however grim things may seem, either internationally, nationally, or in our personal lives, we can hold on to the fact that God is working his purpose out. One day our King will come back and claim his own. I am eagerly awaiting that day!

Reflect on God's kingship over your own life. Confess where you have failed to allow him to reign. Worship him as the King of kings. Cry 'Come, Lord Jesus'.[2]

[1] Wilcock, 1987, p118 [2] Rev 22:20

BIBLE IN A YEAR: **1 Chronicles 7–10; Psalm 68**

INFORMED CHOICE

Health-care professionals provide patients with information about diagnosis, prognosis and treatment options, so that patients can make informed choices. John gives his readers the information they need to make an informed choice about Jesus: 'these are written that you may believe that Jesus is the Messiah'.[1]

These early chapters of John diagnose the human condition and offer a prognosis and treatment plan! The diagnosis is grim: we stand 'condemned' because we have chosen 'darkness' and 'evil' (3:18–20). The prognosis, however, is promising because of Jesus, the giver of both 'light' and 'eternal life' (1:4,5,9; 3:15,16). He alone is the remedy for our sin-sickness. John's Gospel announces the *availability* of this treatment and emphasises the necessity of *availing* ourselves of it. As repeated emphasis on the verb 'believe' suggests (eg 1:12; 2:11; 3:16,36), informed consent is expressed by affirming our trust in Jesus.

John's prologue spells out the fundamental choice that sets sin-sick people on the road to recovering life: 'to all who did receive him, to those who believed in his name, he gave the right to become children of God' (1:12). Varying images present this basic choice: come-and-see invitations, which must be accepted or rejected (1:35–51); welcoming the one to whom the signs point, as opposed to remaining stuck at the signpost (2:11,23,24); being born from above or clinging to familiar things below (3:5–12); being satisfied with temporary thirst-quenchers versus drinking the 'living water' Jesus offers (4:10–15); settling for physical healing as opposed to pursuing wholeness (5:14); craving bread that fills the stomach or feeding on the living bread that satisfies the soul (6:26–58). All these choices have eternal implications: 'while we are free to choose our actions, we are not free to choose the consequences of those actions'.[2] Jesus and John urge us to make not just life-giving but *eternal-life*-giving choices.

Tanya Ferdinandusz

---

[1] John 20:31 [2] Stephen Covey, *The 7 Habits of Highly Effective People*, Simon & Schuster, 2004, p90

Two Word Pictures

Think about the most generous, gracious or exciting invitation you received – how did accepting this invitation affect you?

By using a unique title – 'the Word' – to introduce Jesus, John presents two contrasting word pictures. The first speaks of power, greatness, majesty (vs 1–5). The Word was not just *with* God in his heavenly dwelling, but *was* God (v 1). John's 'In the beginning' echoes Genesis 1:1, transporting us back to that very first beginning. This Word was present even then, powerfully at work in giving form and shape to a formless void and filling it with diverse life forms (v 3). This Word was 'in very nature God' and enjoyed 'equality with God'.[1]

In contrast, the portrayal of the Word as 'flesh' (v 14) connotes weakness, frailty, vulnerability: 'Unimaginably, the Maker of all things shrank down, down, down, so small as to become an ovum, a single fertilised egg barely visible to the naked eye, an egg that would divide and redivide until a foetus took shape, enlarging cell by cell inside a nervous teenager.'[2] In Paul's words, 'he made himself nothing ... being made in human likeness.'[3] The incarnation was this life-giving, darkness-dispelling Word entering a world dominated by death and darkness, offering life and light to a humanity deformed by sin (vs 4,5,9). Yet, the incarnation was no *invasion* but an *invitation*, one humbly given and often rudely rejected – 'his own did not receive him' (v 11).

'He became what we are so that we might become what he is.'[4] The Word through whom everything was created became the crucified one. The Word became vulnerable, that we might enjoy wholeness. Just as, in the beginning, a formless void was given form and filled with teeming life, so a deformed humanity was offered a new beginning – the opportunity to be re-formed in God's likeness, born anew as his own children (vs 12,13).

'Mild he lays his glory by, / born that we no more may die, / born to raise us from the earth, / born to give us second birth.'[5]

---

[1] Phil 2:6 [2] P Yancey, *The Jesus I never knew*, Zondervan, 1995, p36 [3] Phil 2:7 [4] Irenaeus of Lyons, c 130-c 200 [5] C Wesley, 1707–1788, 'Hark! The Herald Angels Sing'

BIBLE IN A YEAR: **1 Chronicles 11–14; Malachi 1,2**

WEDNESDAY 12 JUNE
John 1:19–28

Playing Second Fiddle

How would you respond to the question, 'Who are you?' If God were the one asking the question, would your response be any different?

In an orchestra, the first violins carry the melody. The second violins provide the harmony, which is an important supporting role that makes the melody ring out richer and fuller. When asked which instrument was harder to play, the famous conductor Leonard Bernstein reputedly responded, 'The second fiddle. I can get plenty of first violinists, but to find someone who can play the second fiddle with enthusiasm – that's a problem; and if we have no second fiddle, we have no harmony.'

Today's passage begins with the Jewish leaders peppering John with questions about his identity and role. Both curiosity and controversy surrounded this prophet who had emerged from the Judean desert and quickly made a name for himself as a fearless and forthright preacher. Although influential people had begun to speculate about his identity, John downplayed any hint of celebrity status, promptly vetoing

suggestions that he might be Elijah, Moses or even the Messiah (vs 19–21). When pressed by a high-powered delegation, John's response was plucked straight out of Scripture: 'I am the voice of one calling in the wilderness, "Make straight the way for the Lord"' (v 23).[1] John was *clear* about his identity – both who he was and who he was not. He was *content* in his identity, laying no claims to fame even when presented with a golden opportunity to do so. John was also *confident*. While under no illusion that he was indispensable, John never doubted that his role was important. He was content to be just a 'voice', but he was also a bold, uncompromising and confident voice!

John played second fiddle – and he played it remarkably well. Instead of capitalising on being the centre of attention, he deliberately and purposefully trained the spotlight on Jesus (vs 26,27).

'You're blessed when you're content with just who you are … That's the moment you find yourselves proud owners of everything that can't be bought.'[2]

[1] See Isa 40:3 [2] Matt 5:5, *The Message*

BIBLE IN A YEAR: **1 Chronicles 15,16; Malachi 3,4**

The Chosen One

Lamb of God, you shouldered the weight of my sin, so that I could savour the gift of your peace.

Today's passage includes two titles of Jesus: 'Lamb of God' (v 29) and 'God's Chosen One' (v 34). 'Chosen' usually signifies privilege. As 'God's Chosen One', Jesus fulfilled Isaiah's prophecy: 'Here is my servant ... my chosen one in whom I delight'.[1] Being 'chosen' entails *more* than prestige, position or power. Those chosen *by* God are also chosen *for* God's purposes. Isaiah's prophecy continues, 'he will bring justice to the nations'; this justice, however, was not accomplished by a warrior-king striding forth in might and majesty – 'He will not shout or cry out, or raise his voice in the streets'[2] – but by the blood, sweat and tears of the man John the Baptist introduces as 'the Lamb of God'.

John the Baptist cried, 'Look, the Lamb of God' (v 29). Several decades later, the apostle John was given a vision from God in which he was invited to see that 'the Lion of the tribe of Judah, the Root of David, has triumphed'; yet when John looked, he saw no majestic lion, only 'a Lamb, looking as if it had been slain' yet triumphant 'at the centre of the throne'.[3] God's Chosen One bore the intolerable burden of 'the sin of the world' (v 29) to make available to us, his chosen ones, the immeasurable blessings of salvation. Jesus is both Lamb and Lion, meekness and majesty, Servant and Saviour.

As God's chosen people, we are richly blessed in Christ, who 'takes us to the high places of blessing in him'[4] but, like our Master, we are also chosen to suffer – allowing his refining fire to perfect us in holiness and his potter's wheel to mould us into Christlikeness – and called to step out of our comfort zones and make sacrifices for God's kingdom.

'... you are the ones chosen by God ... God's instruments to do his work and speak out for him.'[5] How well are you doing? How boldly are you speaking out?

[1] Isa 42:1 [2] Isa 42:2 [3] Rev 5:5,6 [4] Eph 1:3, *The Message* [5] 1 Pet 2:9, *The Message*

BIBLE IN A YEAR: **1 Chronicles 17,18; Galatians 1**

John 1:35–42

Abiding Apprenticeship

Invite God to teach you, praying: 'Show me how you work, God; school me in your ways. Take me by the hand; lead me down the path of truth.'[1]

The Greek word that translates as 'disciple' means learner – which may bring to mind students at work in classrooms or in university lecture halls. But the Rabbi-disciple relationship of biblical times was more like the ancient *guru-shishya* (master-disciple) tradition of India and Sri Lanka, where the *shishya* (disciple) was a live-in learner in the home of the *guru* (master). A disciple did not merely learn a trade or craft but also a whole way of life. The master-disciple relationship was central to this learning process, where knowledge and skills were assimilated not by attending a series of lectures but by attending closely to the master's whole lifestyle. Learning involved listening, observing, interacting and imitating.

When Jesus asked two would-be disciples, 'What do you want?', they responded, '... where are you *staying*?' (v 38, emphasis added). The disciples spent quality time with Jesus, not just that day but over many months – listening to him teach, questioning and being questioned, seeing signs and discussing their significance, and observing his interactions with all types of people. Jesus' call, to 'Come' (v 39) and 'Follow' (v 43) was never a command to pursue a curriculum but an invitation to 'be with him'[2] and deepen their relationship with him.

Modern educational institutions frequently focus on filling students with as much information as possible, even offering crash courses that accomplish this in as little time as possible! Formation, unlike filling, is a process that cannot be hurried. Formation that leads to transformation cannot be completed within the confines of the classroom but takes place in all the spaces we inhabit in our everyday lives.

Jesus invites each of us to an intimate and abiding apprenticeship: 'Live in me ... you can't bear fruit unless you are joined with me.'[3]

[1] Ps 25:4,5, *The Message* [2] Mark 3:14 [3] John 15:4, *The Message*

BIBLE IN A YEAR: **1 Chronicles 19–21; Psalm 69**

Unconscious Bias

What do you understand by 'bias'? Do you consider yourself biased? Might hidden biases – that you are not even aware of – be subtly influencing your attitudes and actions?

'Implicit bias refers to the attitudes or stereotypes that affect our understanding, actions and decisions in an unconscious manner … Implicit biases are pervasive. Everyone possesses them, even people with avowed commitments to impartiality such as judges.'[1] Bias itself is not sinful, but claiming to be without bias puts us on shaky ground. Explicit bias, however wrong it may be, is out there on the table, where it can be dealt with, but implicit bias poses a hidden threat since we don't even recognise how such bias shapes our attitudes and influences our interactions.

What about Nathanael? He, like Philip, was eagerly awaiting the Messiah's coming; reference to 'the Law' and 'the prophets' suggests that he was well versed in Scripture (v 45). Jesus himself affirmed that Nathanael was a devout Jew – 'truly … an Israelite' – and a man of integrity, with 'no deceit' (v 47). Nathanael was a good guy, yet he was not free of unconscious bias! The bias seems to burst forth instinctively, without conscious thought: 'Nazareth! Can anything good come from there?' (v 46). Nathanael didn't merely rule out the possibility of the *Messiah* being from Nazareth but went further, with the sweeping assumption that *nothing good* could come from this little village.

Yet, in accepting Philip's gentle, non-confrontational invitation to 'Come and see' (v 46), Nathanael allowed his unconscious bias to be brought to the surface for scrutiny. Imagine what Nathanael might have said about Nazareth *after* meeting Jesus! Not just something 'good', but the very embodiment of goodness had come from Nazareth. In his own home town, Cana, Nathanael would soon witness the glory of Jesus![2]

Learn more about implicit bias. A test like the Implicit Association Test[3] may help you start thinking through your unconscious biases in different areas.

[1] https://kirwaninstitute.osu.edu/article/understanding-implicit-bias [2] John 2:11; 21:2
[3] https://implicit.harvard.edu/implicit/takeatest.html

BIBLE IN A YEAR: **1 Chronicles 22,23; Galatians 2**

Protect Me – Punish Them!

Think about the world news you read or watched recently. How much of this was troubling, terrible, or tragic news? Pick one situation to pray about today.

Today's psalm contains a 'protect me' prayer (vs 1–5) and a 'punish them' prayer (vs 8–11). Both prayers are formulated on the basis of God's character (vs 6,7; 12,13).

The psalmist (probably David) faces attack from 'evildoers' – 'violent', 'wicked', 'arrogant' people (vs 1,4,5). Their actions were deliberate ('devise evil plans'), devious ('set traps'), destructive ('stir up war'); their words were venomous (vs 2–5). David depends for rescue and safety (vs 1,4) on the 'Sovereign LORD', whom he also addresses more personally and intimately as 'my God', 'my strong deliverer' (vs 6,7, emphasis added). The extent of the evil described here recalls Noah's day, when 'every inclination of the thoughts of the human heart was only evil all the time',[1] provoking God's judgement against such terrible wickedness.

A judge's verdict in favour of the innocent party invariably involves punishing the guilty. After his plea for protection, David considers the bigger picture of justice in the land. He knows that evil, if not uprooted and destroyed, 'never to rise' again (v 10), will inevitably take root and 'be established in the land' (v 11). Once again, his prayer is founded on God's character: 'I know that the LORD secures justice for the poor' (v 12). God had already promised, 'It is mine to avenge; I will repay. In due time their foot will slip; their day of disaster is near and their doom rushes upon them'.[2] Though David prays for terrible things to happen to evildoers (vs 9–11), 'these imprecations only repeat in prayer what God had already stated elsewhere would be the fate of those who were impenitent and who were persistently opposing God and his kingdom'.[3] We pray, 'your kingdom come';[4] God's judgement is an inescapable part of this kingdom's coming.

When evil seems to triumph, how will you resist the temptation to get even? Will you turn to God and seek his help to turn the battle over to him?

[1] Gen 6:5 [2] Deut 32:35 [3] Walter Kaiser, *Hard Sayings of the Bible*, IVP, 1996 [4] Matt 6:10

BIBLE IN A YEAR: **1 Chronicles 24–27; Galatians 3**

Transformed by Jesus

Recall signposts – people, conversations, songs, sermons, situations – that marked the road that led you to faith in Jesus. In what ways are you a signpost in another's journey?

Jesus' first sign involved changing water into wine. The bride's family were spared humiliation, and the wedding celebrations continued without disruption. However, this 'first of the signs through which [Jesus] revealed his glory' held far deeper significance, for it resulted in his disciples' belief (v 11) – a saving faith in a Saviour who would bear their sin and shame, and also bless them with abundant life.

In the rich symbolism of the Bible, the number six represents imperfection and inadequacy, while seven signifies perfection and fullness. While it is a contested interpretation, the 'six stone water jars' (v 6) could symbolise Judaism's purification rites, rituals which pointed to important realities but were woefully inadequate fully or permanently to cleanse people of their sin. Filled to the brim, these water jars represented the best that Judaism could offer. The banquet-master's remark, 'you have saved the best till now' (v 10), finds an exciting echo in Hebrews – 'in these last days [God] has spoken to us by his Son', the Son who alone 'provided purification for sins'.[1] Water cleanses and refreshes the body; Jesus purifies and renews the heart. Water is essential for human life; Jesus alone offers 'living water', indispensable for eternal life,[2] and promises 'rivers of living water' flowing from within those who believe in him.[3]

'On the third day' (v 1), Jesus transformed water into wine, a sign that inaugurated his ministry of transformation. On another unforgettable 'third day',[4] Jesus rose from the dead; his resurrection power transforms not just substances but lives: 'if anyone is in Christ, the new creation has come'.[5]

'With joy you will draw water from the wells of salvation.'[6] Lord, draw me into a deeper, stronger relationship with you. Let me never lose my joy in Jesus.

[1] Heb 1:2,3 [2] John 4:10,14 [3] John 7:38 [4] Eg 1 Cor 15:4 [5] 2 Cor 5:17 [6] Isa 12:3

BIBLE IN A YEAR: **1 Chronicles 28,29;** Psalms 70,71

John 2:13–25

A New and Living Way

'The Word became flesh and blood, and moved into the neighbourhood.'[1] Before you read God's Word today, talk to him about what his coming means to you.

Solomon's Temple – the pride and joy of the Jewish people – was rebuilt by Zerubbabel (becoming the Second Temple), after the exiles returned to the land, but many Jews felt that this Temple lacked the 'former glory' of Solomon's Temple.[2] Herod the Great had embarked on an ambitious building project, not only to renovate but also to expand the Temple. This work, which had been going on for 46 years (v 20), was still not over.

The Temple (and, before it, the tabernacle) had always been central in Judaism. There, God's people gathered to praise, plead and be purified of sin. There, God's presence was manifested in a special way in its innermost sanctuary, the Most Holy Place. Temple worship had become corrupt and insular, however. Greedy religious leaders had turned the Temple into a 'market' (v 16) and the traders' occupation of 'the temple courts' (v 14)

hindered Gentiles from worshipping God. Temple reform was certainly necessary, but Jesus came for *more* than reform. Even before the Temple was destroyed by the Romans in AD 70, it was rendered spiritually obsolete and was *replaced* by Jesus, in whom 'all the fullness of the Deity lives in bodily form'.[3]

Jesus replaced this Temple made of stones with himself (v 21) – a body instead of a building, a person instead of a place, with the focus on relationship rather than rituals. All the functions of the Temple now devolve on Jesus. Anyone wanting to praise God, seek forgiveness, obtain 'mercy and … grace to help us in our time of need'[4] – or simply enjoy God's presence – need look no longer to the Temple, with its rituals and priestly mediators. In Jesus, *all* people are invited to enjoy confident access to the Father through this 'new and living way opened for us through … his body.'[5]

'You are the way; thro' you alone / can we the Father find; / in you, O Christ, has God revealed / his heart and will and mind.'[6]

---

[1] John 1:14, *The Message* [2] Hag 2:3 [3] Col 2:9 [4] Heb 4:16 [5] Heb 10:19,20
[6] GW Doane. 1799–1859, 'Thou art the way'

BIBLE IN A YEAR: **2 Chronicles 1,2; Galatians 4**

Ask to Be Born (Again)

What is the most important choice you ever made? Why was this decision so significant?

If you are (or have been) a parent of a teen, you might have heard an indignant, 'Well, I didn't ask to be born!' That's true, of course – no child has a choice in the matter of their birth. Here, however, Jesus told Nicodemus that he must be 'born again' if he wanted to enter God's kingdom (v 3).

At birth, we receive the gift of life and enter this world, but life in God and in his kingdom does not accrue to anyone as a birthright. It requires a choice: 'to all who did receive him, to those who believed in his name, he gave the right to become children of God'.[1] Preconditions are intertwined in this choice – we must 'receive' and 'believe' in Jesus in order to be 'born of God'[2] and become his children. Just as physical birth makes us members of an earthly family and citizens of a country, this spiritual birth not only includes us in God's family but also makes us citizens of his kingdom. This was the life-giving truth that Jesus wanted Nicodemus to appreciate when he emphasised the necessity of being 'born again' (v 3) and 'born of water and the Spirit' (v 5). 'Water' probably denotes repentance – a 180-degree turnabout, representing a complete reorientation of our lives. The 'Spirit' signifies relationship, since 'the Spirit you received brought about your adoption to sonship' and it is by this Spirit that 'we cry, "*Abba*, Father"'.[3]

None of us *asked* to be born. But *all* of us can ask to be born from above. Yet, many refuse to do so. Jesus lamented, 'you people do not accept our testimony' (v 11). *The Message* puts it like this: 'Yet instead of facing the evidence and accepting it, you procrastinate with questions.'

Holy Spirit, help those who are grappling with God-questions, that they may be convinced by the mounting evidence of his love, power and grace.

[1] John 1:12 [2] John 1:13 [3] Rom 8:15

BIBLE IN A YEAR: **2 Chronicles 3–5; Galatians 5**

John 3:16–21

Choose the Son-Light

'The people walking in darkness have seen a great light; on those living in the land of deep darkness a light has dawned.'[1] Praise Jesus, the Light.

In art, literature, philosophy and theology, darkness frequently symbolises ignorance, lies or evil, while light represents knowledge, truth or holiness. In John's Gospel, Jesus is repeatedly depicted as the true Light.[2] The announcement 'light has come into the world' sounds a joyous note of hope, but John's reference to this as a 'verdict' also recalls us to its darker side (v 19).

Despite its many positive associations, we are sometimes uncomfortable and ill at ease in the light. After being in darkness for an extended period, the human eye takes time to adapt to exposure. We may screw up our eyes in protest or shade our eyes from the light source. Some people suffer from light sensitivity, unable to tolerate the level of light in the environment. Today's passage deals with people so accustomed to spiritual darkness that they have grown to love this darkness – representing the shadier side of life – and refuse to step into the light (vs 19,20). Since light exposes what darkness conveniently covers up, it is a hard and humbling process to come into the light. Both literally and metaphorically, darkness may become our comfort zone. Nicodemus, for instance, came to Jesus under cover of darkness (v 2), perhaps fearing to be too closely associated with the increasingly controversial figure of Jesus of Nazareth. This prominent Pharisee was in the dark about the spiritual truths Jesus proclaimed (vs 10–12) and, by the end of their discussion, Nicodemus did not appear to have stepped into the light – although he did do so later on.[3]

Both in the physical and spiritual realms light and life are inextricably linked. The *sun*, which generates heat, light and energy, is essential for sustaining physical life; the *Son* – source and substance of light and life – is indispensable for eternal life (v 18).

'We are as much afraid in the light as children in the dark.'[4] Are you resisting Jesus, the true Light, in any areas of your life?

---

[1] Isa 9:2 [2] John 1:4,5,9; 8:12; 9:5 [3] John 19:38-42
[4] Seneca, paraphrasing Lucretius, https://en.wikiquote.org/wiki/Plato

BIBLE IN A YEAR: **2 Chronicles 6,7; Galatians 6**

The Best Man

How would you define 'greatness'? How do you think God defines 'greatness'?

As I think about the last few weddings I attended, I can picture the bride, I can recall, more sketchily, the bridegroom, but the best man is just a blur! Despite his lofty title, the 'best' man seldom receives much attention! And rightly so.

John the Baptist stood in the position of 'best man' to Jesus, the Bridegroom, but some of John's disciples were unhappy about attention being diverted away from John. Their words seem designed to fan the flames of rivalry: 'the one you testified about – look, he is baptising, and everyone is going to him' (v 26). Such words might easily have provoked insecurity, envy or resentment. Baptising was John's speciality – the very name by which we know him, 'John the Baptist', derived from it! John's disciples, like many of us today, measured success by numbers – 'everyone is going to him'. Yet, although his position as market leader[1] seemed to be slipping away, John did not view this as a threat or interpret it as failure.

There is not even the trace of a competitive streak in John; instead, we see a spirit of humble and joyful contentment in his assertions that 'A person can receive only what is given them from heaven' (v 27) and 'I am not the Messiah but am sent ahead of him' (v 28). John's job was waiting and listening for the bridegroom (v 29); he was neither threatened nor diminished by this second-fiddle role but found in it his richest and truest fulfilment. Jesus commended John: 'among those born of women there has not risen anyone greater than John the Baptist'.[2] John's greatness lay in becoming 'less' so that Jesus would become 'greater' (v 30). He was a great 'best man' because he recognised who was *truly* best and then gave *his* best to proclaim the greatness of Jesus.

Ask yourself: 'In all that I say and do, and in how I live, do I make Jesus look good?'

[1] See Mark 1:5 [2] Matt 11:11

BIBLE IN A YEAR: **2 Chronicles 8,9; Psalm 72**

John 4:1–15

Living Water for All

'As the deer pants for streams of water, so my soul pants for you, my God. My soul thirsts for God, for the living God.'¹

We all need water to live. In 2015, one of the United Nations' targets was to 'achieve universal and equitable access to safe and affordable drinking water for all' by 2030. By 2020, 74% of the global population had access to 'safely managed drinking water', so a quarter of the world (around two billion people) still did *not* enjoy safe water.

In Bible times, too, access to safe drinking water was a matter of concern. Jesus' conversation with the woman at the well began with a simple request for a drink – and developed into a discussion about 'living water' (v 10) and spiritual thirst. Living water symbolises the Holy Spirit,² through whom we enter into the only relationship that can fully and permanently satisfy our most fundamental thirst. Whereas water is essential for life, living water is indispensable for eternal life. The God who 'so loved the world that he gave his one and only Son'³ made salvation available for all. Jesus offers living water to anyone who asks (v 10).

At the physical level, Jesus experienced thirst – at Samaria, after a tiring journey, in the noonday sun (v 6); and again, at Golgotha, after being whipped, scourged and nailed to the cross. At a deeper and far more agonising level, Jesus thirsted for the salvation of the world. The cross – from upon which he cried out through cracked and parched lips, 'I am thirsty'⁴ – was the terrible cost he bore to make this living water freely available to all people. The encounter that began with Jesus asking for a drink of water concluded with many in Samaria confessing, 'we know that this man really is the Saviour of the world' (v 42). The goal of living water for all had *begun* to be realised!

Lord, help me to consciously and consistently cultivate a thirst for you.

---

¹ Ps 42:1,2 ² John 7:37–39 ³ John 3:16 ⁴ John 19:28

BIBLE IN A YEAR: **2 Chronicles 10–12; Ephesians 1**

Protect Me – from Me!

'Turn your eyes upon Jesus, / look full in his wonderful face, / and the things of earth will grow strangely dim, / in the light of his glory and grace.'[1]

As in last Sunday's psalm, the psalmist (probably David) prays for protection. Here, however, he does not plead for protection from *enemies* but protection from *himself*. '… if you think you are standing firm, be careful that you don't fall!'[2] While alert to the wickedness around him, David recognises his own inclination to evil. His prayer for protection is urgent – 'come quickly' (v 1) – and contains a three-pronged defence strategy involving self (vs 3,4), others (v 5) and God (v 8).

David seeks God's help to set up safeguards to protect himself from himself! He begins with the mouth. James describes the tongue's dangerous power and our own inability to control it: 'We get it wrong nearly every time we open our mouths.'[3] We need 'a guard' over our mouths (v 3) lest our words 'ruin the world, turn harmony to chaos, throw mud on a reputation, send the whole world up in smoke and go up in smoke with it'![4] David recognises how swift the journey is from what the heart is 'drawn to' to what the hands decide to dabble in; so he pleads for protection for his heart (v 4a) and strength to resist the tempting 'delicacies' before him (v 4b).

To eat with someone signifies table fellowship, which is not just sharing a meal but implies belonging and shared beliefs. We can and must nurture friendships with unbelievers, but our mentors and influencers must be prayerfully chosen. David resisted the intimacy of table fellowship with evildoers and held himself accountable to the 'righteous' (v 5). Secret sins exert a stranglehold on us; talking through our struggles with mature believers can help to loosen sin's iron grip but, above all other safeguards and sources of help, David's surest defence was to fix his gaze on God and seek refuge in him (v 8).

Our Father in heaven, 'Keep us safe from ourselves and the Devil.'[5]

[1] Helen Lemmel, 1863–1961 [2] 1 Cor 10:12 [3] James 3:2, *The Message* [4] James 3:5,6, *The Message*
[5] Matt 6:13, *The Message*

BIBLE IN A YEAR: **2 Chronicles 13–15; Ephesians 2**

John 4:16–30

Care-fronting

Consider: Do you view speaking truth and showing love as an either/ or option or as a both/and package?

In his book *Caring Enough to Confront*, David Augsburger coins the term 'care-fronting', which marries the need for love (caring) with the need for truth (confronting). He writes: 'Care-fronting is offering genuine caring that lifts, supports, and encourages the other. (To care is to bid another to grow, to welcome, invite, and support growth in another.) Care-fronting is being upfront with important facts that can call out new awareness, insight and understanding. (To confront effectively is to offer the maximum of useful information with the minimum of threat and stress.)'[1]

Jesus' encounter with the Samaritan woman illustrates care-fronting at its finest! She was scorned by the Jews because of her race and probably shunned by her own community because of her lifestyle. The rarity of the respect shown by Jesus probably prompted her startled rejoinder: 'You are a Jew and I am a Samaritan woman. How can you ask me for a drink?' (v 9). As she drew water from the well, Jesus drew her into conversation, confronting her with important truths about God, spiritual thirst, worship, her own lifestyle and himself.

Augsburger writes, 'If I love you, I must tell you the truth … Will you hear love in my truth?'[2] When Jesus spoke truth, the woman *heard* his love and *responded* by confessing, 'I have no husband' (v 17). Those who choose to remain in darkness 'will not come into the light for fear that their deeds will be exposed'.[3] This woman, however, when care-fronted by Jesus, ventured out from the shadows and stepped into the light, not only allowing her deeds to be exposed but even proclaiming publicly, 'Come, see a man who told me everything I've ever done. Could this be the Messiah?' (v 29).

Seek God's strength to voice hard but necessary truths. Pray for gentleness and sensitivity to temper your truth-telling with love.

---

[1] David Augsburger, *Caring Enough to Confront*, third edition, Revell, 2014, p10
[2] Augsburger, 2014, front matter [3] John 3:20

BIBLE IN A YEAR: **2 Chronicles 16,17; Psalm 73**

Break The Bias

Have you – or someone close to you – been discriminated against because of race, religion, gender, social status, or some other factor? How did this make you feel?

In the unfolding story, the despised Samaritans come out looking better than Jesus' Jewish disciples. A Samaritan woman had responded enthusiastically to Jesus' invitation to drink of living water and she set out eagerly to share this news with her fellow Samaritans (vs 28–30). The Jewish disciples were 'surprised to find him talking with a woman' (v 27), particularly a Samaritan woman. Yet none of them dared to voice the questions that must have troubled them: '"What do you want?" or "Why are you talking with her?"' Sidestepping the controversy between Jews and Samaritans (see v 9), the disciples opted for a safer topic: 'Rabbi, eat something' (v 31). Just as he had used the metaphor of water to teach about spiritual thirst, Jesus used this remark about food to explain his deepest hunger: his desire to do the Father's will and 'finish his work' (v 34) – work which included a Samaritan harvest.

Traditionally, the Jews viewed the Samaritans with dislike, distrust and even disgust. Jesus challenged his disciples to break the bias by looking through the lens of God's perspective and purposes rather than their own prejudices: 'I tell you, open your eyes and look at the fields! They are ripe for harvest' (v 35). And it would be a *rich* harvest! Because of a Samaritan woman's faithful testimony – which, incidentally, parallels the 'come and see' approach of the early Jewish disciples[1] – many Samaritans heard about Jesus and were already heading towards him. From the lips of these despised Samaritans would come one of the most powerful testimonies about Jesus: 'this man really is the Saviour of the world' (v 42).

In what ways is God challenging you to break the bias?

[1] See John 1:35–46

BIBLE IN A YEAR: **2 Chronicles 18–20; Ephesians 3**

John 4:43-54

Don't Be Sign-Dependent

Think about an occasion when you became deeply conscious of God's presence in your life. How did you respond? Talk to God now about this experience.

Following a fruitful stay in Samaria, Jesus was back in home territory. Although 'the Galileans welcomed him' (v 45), it was not the kind of reception the Samaritans had given Jesus. The Samaritans had believed in Jesus 'because of his words' (v 41), *without* the benefit of miracles; but the Galileans, having seen the signs Jesus performed in Jerusalem at the Passover Festival (v 45), were clearly hoping for more of the same. They sought more miracles, not a relationship with the Messiah.

Signs were significant in Jesus' ministry. In this Gospel's purpose statement, John explains that he recorded these signs so that 'you may believe that Jesus is the Messiah ... that by believing you may have life in his name'.[1] Although many in Jerusalem had seen his signs and believed in his name, 'Jesus would not entrust himself to them, for he knew all people'.[2] He knew that their professions of faith were shallow, not progressing beyond the sign to the one to whom the sign pointed. Similarly, Jesus criticised the Galileans because they required a steady diet of signs and wonders to sustain their belief (v 48).

The royal official also sought a sign. What drove him to Jesus was not faith but despair over his dying son (vs 46,47). Yet, when Jesus declined to accompany him and simply instructed him to go home, assuring him that his son would live, 'The man took Jesus at his word' and obeyed (v 50). When the sign materialised – and his son was healed – he was able to 'realise' the wonder of what Jesus had done (vs 52,53). For the Galilean crowds, signs were endpoints; but for the official, the sign was a starting point, a springboard to a deeper faith, one that he, like the Samaritan woman, also shared with those around him (v 53).

Saviour, help me to keep on seeking you with all my heart, understanding that you yourself are the most precious sign of all.

[1] John 20:31 [2] John 2:23,24

BIBLE IN A YEAR: **2 Chronicles 21–23; Ephesians 4**

Healed, but not Holy

'Long before he laid down earth's foundations, he had us in mind, had settled on us as the focus of his love, to be made whole and holy'.[1]

'Do you want to get well?' seems a strange question to ask someone who had been an invalid for 38 years (vs 5,6). The answer is obvious – *or is it?* Jesus' question went unanswered. Instead of responding enthusiatically, the invalid began grumbling about his helplessness (v 7). Had the years chipped away at his hope and made him cynical? Had he settled so deeply into a victim mentality that even *discomfort* had somehow become a comfort zone? While *we* may view grumbling as a minor attitude problem, the Israelites' wilderness narratives show that God regards grumbling as a serious sin.[2] Grumbling gets in the way of contentment; since grumbling is ungracious, it also impedes grace.

The World Health Organisation defines health as 'a state of complete physical, mental and social well-being and not merely the absence of disease or infirmity'.

Medical science testifies to the powerful interconnectedness of physical well-being and the state of our mind, emotions and even our spiritual state. True wellness involves wholeness of the whole person. Although Jesus had cured the man in body (vs 8,9), he was not made whole. Despite being well again, he was not out of danger. The command to 'Stop sinning' (v 14) does not imply that the man's sin had *caused* his sickness; rather, Jesus was warning him that a settled lifestyle of sin had consequences far worse than any physical disability. While the man's sins are not named, he comes across as self-absorbed and ungrateful – for he made no attempt to discover his healer's identity and offer thanks. He even tattled about Jesus to the Jewish leaders (v 15)! Nevertheless, Jesus sought him out, longing to complete his work of healing. It is this pursuit of our holiness that keeps the Father and Jesus always 'working' (v 17).

Do you long for wholeness? Are you committed to holiness?

[1] Eph 1:4, *The Message* [2] Exod 14:11,12; 15:22–24; 16:1–3; 17:1–3

BIBLE IN A YEAR: **2 Chronicles 24,25; Ephesians 5**

John 5:16–30

No Hierarchy

'Don't push your way to the front; don't sweet-talk your way to the top. Put yourself aside, and help others get ahead.'[1] How difficult is this?

The Jewish leaders accused Jesus of 'making himself equal with God' (v 18). They viewed this as rebellion, but the equality Jesus claimed was not one that attempts or even *needs* to prove itself better, faster or stronger! Hierarchies rank people in order of importance or power, and people usually seek upward mobility within a hierarchy to gain *more* power, honour or glory. This human model of hierarchy, however, does not explain how the Trinity operates and relates. Although he was sent by the Father, the Son does not rank lower than the Father. Between Father and Son (and Spirit), there is no power struggle. Their equality simply *is* – and does not have to be fought for or defended.

The legal term 'jointly and severally' (meaning, both together and separately) denotes that each person in a partnership shares rights and responsibilities equally.

Father and Son operate 'jointly and severally' in the work they engage in (v 19) and the authority they exercise (vs 21,22,26,27), within a relationship rooted in a love that is untainted by rivalry (v 20). The Son always acts in accordance with the Father's will and his will is also in perfect accord with the Father's. The Son does not simply exercise delegated authority, but enjoys true power-sharing. Neither acts independently – for one to act is for *both* to act (v 19). The Son's dependence (v 19) is never demeaning, just as the Father's sending is never authoritarian.

Within the Godhead, there *is* no 'greater' – there is only loving, honouring and glorifying one another, while working together in perfect harmony.

What do you learn from the Trinity about living in community?

[1] Phil 2:3, *The Message*

BIBLE IN A YEAR: **2 Chronicles 26–28; Psalm 74**

John 5:31–47

A Case for Christ

What objections to faith in Christ are voiced by people around you? Seek God's wisdom to build a case for Christ that looks at both God's world and his Word.

When Lewis Carroll's Alice declares that 'one cannot believe impossible things', the Queen responds: 'I daresay you haven't had much practice ... When I was your age, I always did it for half-an-hour a day. Why, sometimes I've believed as many as six impossible things before breakfast'.[1] People sometimes think that being a Christian requires believing in the impossible and the improbable, but faith in Jesus does not mean abandoning reason; in fact, today's passage shows how *reasonable* it is to believe in Jesus.

The Jewish leaders had opposed Jesus' claim to be 'equal with God' (v 18). Jesus now builds a solid case in support of his claim. His first witness was John the Baptist. When questioned by a delegation sent by the Jewish leadership, John had 'testified to the truth' (v 33).[2] The signs Jesus performed serve as exhibit one in this case for Christ. As Nicodemus had observed,[3] these signs were evidence of God's power at work in Jesus (v 36); the signs also pointed to Jesus' identity, as in Cana, where 'his disciples believed in him'.[4] The Father, the star witness in this case, had 'testified' about Jesus (v 37) – this might have pointed to God's public and audible testimony at Jesus' baptism and transfiguration, but probably also referred to the dual witness of Scripture and conscience. Jesus also cited the testimony of Scripture – an expert witness relied on heavily by the Jews themselves (v 39). Nevertheless, despite the mounting evidence, Jesus' opponents refused to 'believe' or 'accept' the one sent by God (vs 38,43). By refusing to receive and believe in the true light of the world, they opted to remain in darkness.

'Faith is not a question of shutting our eyes ... It is a leap, but a leap into the light and not a leap into the dark.'[5]

---

[1] Lewis Carroll, *Through the Looking-Glass and What Alice Found There*, Evertype, 2009, p68
[2] John 1:19–27 [3] John 3:2 [4] John 2:11 [5] J Polkinghorne, *Serious Talk*, Trinity Press, 1995, p1

BIBLE IN A YEAR: **2 Chronicles 29,30; Ephesians 6**

Psalm 142

Groaning before God

'God's Spirit ... does our praying in and for us, making prayer out of our wordless sighs, our aching groans.'[1] Invite the Holy Spirit to shape your prayer today.

Today's psalm was a prayer of David 'When he was in the cave'. During his difficult years as a fugitive, David often sought refuge in caves. Perhaps this psalm was composed when David fled from Gath to the cave of Adullam.[2]

The man at Bethesda had 'no one to help me into the pool';[3] thrice in this psalm David laments that there is 'no one' to help or care about him (v 4). David's 'complaint' (v 2), however, is not in the same category as the grumbling of the man at the pool! David does not grumble so much as *groan* before God. In this outpouring of feelings, as to a trusted confidant, nothing is bottled up or buried; everything is brought boldly – and loudly! – before God (vs 1–4). When hemmed in by troubles, we naturally yearn for the comforting warmth of a friendly presence. Even Jesus experienced this longing in the hours before his crucifixion: 'My soul is overwhelmed with sorrow to the point of death. Stay here and keep watch with me.'[4] David was keenly aware of his own frailty – 'my spirit grows faint within me' (v 3); Kidner comments, 'the strain of being hated and hunted is almost too much, and faith is at full stretch'.[5] That safe space in which he felt free to break down before God was probably what saved David from a nervous breakdown!

Groaning before God also readied David for higher ground. From *feeling* that he had 'no refuge' (v 4), David progresses to affirming *facts* and *faith* – God is not merely a refuge but '*my* refuge' (v 5, emphasis added). Although the 'desperate need' (v 6) remains, David *himself* is no longer desperate. The prayer that began on a note of panic ends on a high note of hopeful praise and trust (v 7).

Your feelings of hopelessness and helplessness, presented to God and processed in God's presence, can be transformed by his grace.

[1] Rom 8:26, *The Message* [2] 1 Sam 22:1 [3] John 5:7 [4] Matt 26:38
[5] Derek Kidner, *Psalms 73–150*, IVP, 1975 (reprinted 2007), p473

BIBLE IN A YEAR: **2 Chronicles 31,32; Luke 1:1–38**